Teaching Terrific 5's

TEACHING Terrific 5's

and other children

Ray Langstrom, MA   Jane Hodges, PhD

Green Dragon Books
Lake Worth, FL

Green Dragon Books
P.O. Box 1608
Lake Worth, FL 33460

Teaching Terrific Fives
A Green Dragon Books Publication

© 2013 by Green Dragon Books
© 2008 by Brumby Holdings, LLC

No part of this book may be reproduced or transmitted in any form or by any means, electronic or mechanical, including photocopying, recording, or by any information storage and retrieval system, without written permission from the publisher. For information, address Green Dragon Books.

Green Dragon is a trademark of Green Dragon Books , consisting of a special identifiable green and unique dragon which is expressingly individual to the publisher. This work is registered with the U.S. Patent and Trademark Office and in other countries.

Green Dragon Books
P.O. Box 1608
Lake Worth, FL 33460

Printed in the United States of America and the United Kingdom.

Library of Congress Control Number: 2008925561

ISBN (Paperback): 0-89334-449-4
ISBN (Hardcover): 0-89334-448-6

Book design & layout: Marcia Karasoff

Contents

INTRODUCTION
   Welcome to Teaching Terrific 5's 2
   Developmental Stages for 5's 5

ACTIVITIES
   Social/Emotional Development 9
      Standing My Ground (Protects Self) 10
      Care to Be Fair (Shows Concern for Fairness) 16
      You Can Count on Me (Shows Responsibility) 21
      Should I, Shouldn't I (Shows Awareness of Consequences) 25
      Express It Out Loud (Shows Creativity) 31
      The Best Me I Can Be (Shows Appropriate Values) 36
      Finding Friends (Makes Friends) 40
      The Many Colors of Me (Has Varying Emotions) 44

   Language Development 53
      Do Tell (Sequences and Retells) 54
      Picture This (Shows Reading Interest) 59
      Reader Ready (Knows Reading Progression) 63
      Now I Know My ABC's (Knows Alphabet) 67
      Out of My Head (Uses Imagination) 80
      If I Were You (Plays Roles) 85
      Knock, Knock, Tick, Tock (Discriminates Consonants) 92
      You Can Say That Again (Speaks Informally) 100

   Cognitive Development 107
      'Tis the Season (Knows Seasons) 108
      Pencil Portrait (Draws Person) 112
      You're Out of Order (Classifies Objects) 114
      Are You for Real? (Recognizes Fantasy) 116
      What If (Recognizes Cause and Effect) 118
      Who Knew (Predicts outcomes) 122
      What's in a Year (Identifies Months) 127
      Look at the Time (Recognizes Clock Numbers) 129

   Motor Skills Development 133
      Piece It Together (Works Puzzle) 134
      Cut it Out (Uses Scissors) 137
      Copying Capitals (Copies Uppercase Letters) 140
      Skip Around (Skips) 149

Contents

Motor Skills Development (Cont'd)
    Heads Up! (Catches Ball) 152
    Back It Up (Walks Backwards) 154
    Write On! (Copies All Letters) 156
    Family Portrait (Draws People) 160

Hygiene/ Self-Help Development 165
    Take a Taste (Tries New Food) 166
    What's to Eat (Identifies Food) 171
    Play It Safe (Shows Safety Judgment) 176
    How's the Weather (Recognizes Weather) 182
    Coming and Going (Understands Travel) 185
    No Place Like Home (Knows Address/Phone Number) 189
    Ready to Wear (Dresses Self) 197
    Table Tools (Uses Spoon and Fork) 201

BONUS MATERIAL
  Common Core Standards Correlations 205
  Humanics National Child Assessment Form 209

Introduction

Introduction

WELCOME!

If you're reading this book, it's likely you're interested in applying practical classroom or home activities to help strengthen your five-year-old's developmental growth in a number of different areas. You want to sharpen your own understanding of the skills and behaviors typically present in a five year-old child. And you're looking for the materials and activities that will help you reinforce and develop those skills and behaviors in the most positive and effective way. Used alone, this activity book will guide you through the five important developmental areas:

- **Social/Emotional**
- **Language**
- **Cognitive**
- **Motor Skills**
- **Hygiene/Self-Help**

The book provides fun and engaging goal-oriented activities designed to encourage a child's progress in each developmental area.

TAKE YOUR TEACHING TO THE NEXT LEVEL!

Use this book together with the *HUMANICS NATIONAL CHILD ASSESSMENT FORM* (HNCAF) to take your understanding of preschool enrichment to the next level. The HNCAF is a checklist of skills and behaviors a child is likely to develop in a given year of life. Implicit in the checklist is the understanding that, like snowflakes, no two children are exactly alike. Each child's individual growth and development should be closely considered within the broader framework of the assessment.

Recording observations about an individual child (and how s/he progresses through the activities in this book) will provide parents and teachers with a Child Development Profile - a visual representation of the child's evolution across the five critical developmental areas. The Profile will prove to be an invaluable tool for designing an educational experience that will respond to and stimulate the individual nature and personality of the child.

Introduction

Above all else, have FUN with these activities, pay close attention to your kids, teach with passion, and you can't go wrong. ENJOY!

WHAT YOU'LL FIND IN THIS BOOK

Easy-to-Follow Outline of Developmental Areas

Teaching Terrific 5's is divided into five units that correspond to each of the developmental areas you'll observe in your five-year-olds:

- **Social/Emotional**
- **Language**
- **Cognitive**
- **Motor Skills**
- **Hygiene/Self-Help**

Each unit is further broken down into eight sections based on the eight characteristics (skills and behaviors) likely to be present in a child this age. These correspond the skills and behaviors found on the HNCAF checklist.

Enrichment Activities

For each skill/behavior, there are corresponding activities that provide fun and stimulating learning for the child. And, because the activities are synchronized with the HNCAF, they provide an efficient way to keep your checklist as you advance through the book. This observing and recording a child's progress with each activity will help you gauge their development in each area, and determine their readiness for advancing to the next level.

Goals

Each activity sets specific goals to be accomplished. A child's ability to meet each goal will help you determine whether a characteristic is apparent and to what degree.

Mind Stretchers

Because each child progresses at an individual pace, *Mind Stretchers* are included with each activity to help you provide the right level of learning for a child's developing skill set. Look for the Budding Learner and Blossoming Learner icons below to guide you.

Introduction

 = *a Budding Learner in the early stages of development and who is most comfortable with basic activities*

 = *a Blossoming Learner at a peak stage of development and who is ready to take on a bigger challenge*

Teacher Tips

Many activities also include ***Teacher Tips*** that give ideas for tailoring an activity to the varying sizes and capabilities of different classroom environments.

> *The art of teaching is the art of assisting discovery.*
>
> *--Mark Van Doren*

Introduction

DEVELOPMENTAL STAGES FOR 5'S

SOCIAL / EMOTIONAL

Protects Self
Stands up for own rights and does not permit others to take unfair advantage.

Shows Concern for Fairness
Plays fairly and cares what happens to other children.

Shows Responsibility
Takes responsibility for own behavior; stays within the rules of games and activities.

Aware of Consequences
Shows awareness of likely outcomes of behavior.

Shows Creativity
Offers original ideas; shows flexibility and creativity in play.

Shows Appropriate Values
Shows consideration, sense of humor and self-discipline.

Makes Friends
Finds and makes friends easily.

Shows Varying Emotions
Alternates between acting amenable and assertive.

LANGUAGE

Sequences and Retells
Retells a simple story in sequence.

Shows Reading Interest
"Reads" a picture story book.

Knows Reading Progression
Knows and exhibits appropriate reading progressions from left to right and top to bottom.

Knows Alphabet
Recognizes and names letters of the alphabet on sight.

Uses Imagination
Creates simple stories with logical sequence.

Plays Roles
Play involves pretending to be another recognizable person.

Discriminates Consonants
Recognizes and names beginning and ending consonants sounds of a word.

Speaks Informally
Uses slang and clichés.

Introduction

DEVELOPMENTAL STAGES FOR 5'S

COGNITIVE

Knows Seasons
Knows seasons and their relation to events and holidays.

Draws Person
Draws human figure with details.

Classifies Objects
Sorts objects into sets according to use.

Recognizes Fantasy
Distinguishes between fantasy and reality.

Recognizes Cause and Effect
Knows relationship between an action and its cause.

Predicts Outcomes
Anticipates consequences of simple actions.

Identifies Months
Identifies calendar months according to seasons.

Recognizes Clock Numbers
Identifies and names numbers on a clock.

MOTOR SKILLS

Works Puzzle
Successfully assembles a simple five-piece puzzle.

Uses Scissors
Cuts with scissors smoothly and with moderate control; cuts on a drawn line.

Copies Uppercase Letters
Copies large capital letters.

Skips
Skips continuously for a defined distance.

Catches Ball
Catches 3"-4" thrown ball using hands only.

Walks Backward
Walks backward in a defined space without bumping others.

Copies All Letters
Copies letters uniformly according to height.

Draws
Draws human figures and other objects close to scale.

Introduction

DEVELOPMENTAL STAGES FOR 5'S

HYGIENE / SELF-HELP

Tries New Food
Samples new food when served.

Identifies Food
Classifies foods according to nutritional value.

Shows Safety Judgment
Makes smart choices that show an understanding of safety.

Recognizes Weather
Understands weather concepts; identifies play activities suitable for weather conditions; dresses appropriately for the weather.

Understands Travel
Locates classroom in the morning; knows afternoon pick-up routine.

Knows Address/Phone Number
Knows home address or location; knows phone number for home or responsible adult.

Dresses Self
Dresses self and ties own shoes.

Uses Spoon and Fork
Uses eating utensils with some help from fingers.

A good teacher is like a candle — it consumes itself to light the way of others.

--*Author Unknown*

Social Emotional

UNIT 1
Developmental Activities

Standing My Ground
Protects self

Care to be Fair
Shows concern for fairness

You Can Count on Me
Shows responsibility

Should I, Shouldn't I
Shows awareness of consequences

Express It Out Loud
Shows creativity

The Best Me I Can Be
Shows appropriate values

Finding Friends
Makes friends

The Many Colors Of Me
Shows varying emotions

Social Emotional

STANDING MY GROUND
Protects Self

The mighty oak was once a little nut that stood its ground

Social Emotional

STANDING MY GROUND
Protects Self

Activity 1
Acorn-and-Oak Discussion

Goal
Know what it means to "stand my ground."

- **Share** the acorn/oak quote: The mighty oak was once a little nut that stood its ground.

- **Talk** about what the statement means in the most literal sense: An acorn is a seed that plants itself firmly in the ground — braving the wind and rain — in order to take root and become a tree.

- **Invite** children to think of ways they may have to "stand their ground." The acorn faces many challenges (weather, foot traffic, etc.) What kinds of challenges do YOU face (on the playground, in the classroom, at home)? How can you be strong and stand up to these challenges? (e.g., bullies, other kids who play unfairly, etc.)

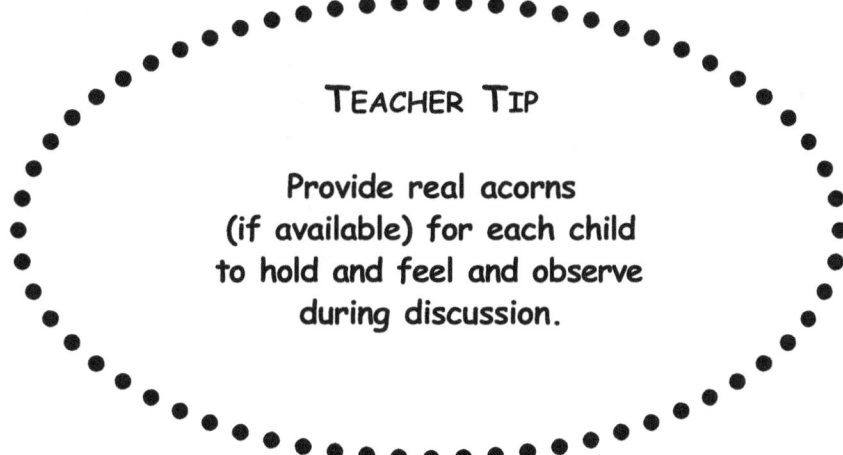

TEACHER TIP

Provide real acorns (if available) for each child to hold and feel and observe during discussion.

Social Emotional

STANDING MY GROUND
Protects Self

Activity 2
Acorn-and-Oak Role Play

Goal
Know how to protect myself and stand up for my rights

- Have children decorate their own "acorn caps" (brown flat-bottomed coffee filters) with crayons, glitter, buttons, stickers, etc. Encourage kids to be creative! Each cap should express the "acorn's" individual personality. Children should wear acorn caps for the duration of Activity 2.

- "Oak tree" (teacher) faces the "acorns," and says: "Today I'm a mighty oak, but when I was an acorn, sometimes people picked on me. How do you think I stood my ground?"

- Call upon "acorns" for answers to the following:

    How should I stand my ground if someone says ...
    - I don't like you anymore.
    - Your idea is stupid.
    - You can't play with me .

Social Emotional

STANDING MY GROUND
Protects Self

● Suggest answers to questions that show both confidence and courtesy.

- I won't listen to unkind words
- You shouldn't talk to me that way.
- Your idea is good, but so is mine. Let's find a way to use them both together.
- If you change your mind, I'll still play with you.

● **Praise** "acorns" who give confident and courteous answers by saying, for example:

(Alex) is doing a great job of standing his ground. He's sure to grow into a mighty oak tree.

- Sure!
- Can I join your team?

● **Remind** "acorns" that confident people speak clearly and directly.

- Speak loudly enough to be heard.
- Express your thoughts clearly and directly.
- Look in people's eyes.

Have "acorns" practice speaking this way

MIND STRETCHERS

Budding Learners:
Offer a choice of different responses to the questions at left. Ask budding learners to decide which are good "acorn" answers.

Blossoming Learners:
Allow blossoming learners to make up their own original "acorn answers." Invite them to demonstrate for the group.

Social Emotional

STANDING MY GROUND

Protects Self

Activity 3
Planting Acorns

Goal
Understand how an acorn grows into a tree

- Copy labels on following page. Add children's names and attach to their acorn cups.

- Use a pencil to poke a hole in the bottom of a Styrofoam cup.

- Fill the cup with potting soil.

- Set an acorn on top of the soil, covering it halfway.

- Place the cup on a small tray or saucer so the water can drain.

- Add enough water to moisten the soil. Water once every week to keep the soil from drying out.

- Watch acorn trees grow! (The first sign of a stem should appear in just a few weeks.)

Social Emotional

STANDING MY GROUND
Protects Self

Copy labels below. Add children's names and attach to their acorn cups.

_____ I'M STANDING MY GROUND	_____ I'M STANDING MY GROUND
_____ I'M STANDING MY GROUND	_____ I'M STANDING MY GROUND
_____ I'M STANDING MY GROUND	_____ I'M STANDING MY GROUND
_____ I'M STANDING MY GROUND	_____ I'M STANDING MY GROUND
_____ I'M STANDING MY GROUND	_____ I'M STANDING MY GROUND
_____ I'M STANDING MY GROUND	_____ I'M STANDING MY GROUND

Social Emotional

CARE TO BE FAIR
Shows Concern for Fairness

LET'S SING!

FRIENDLY WENDELL

(Sung to the tune of *SKIP TO MY LOU*)

Wendell is a teddy bear.
When he plays, he's fair, fair, fair.
Wendell is a caring bear.
That's what makes him friendly.

Wendell likes to share, share, share.
When is friends need help, he's there.
Wendell is a helpful bear.
That's what makes him friendly.

Just like Wendell, I can share.
Just like Wendell, I play fair.
That is how I show I care.
That's what makes me friendly.

Social Emotional

CARE TO BE FAIR
Shows Concern for Fairness

Activity 1
Meet FRIENDLY WENDELL

Goal
Understand that playing fair makes a good friend

- **Sing** the FRIENDLY WENDELL song on the previous page. Then talk about . . .

    - Why is it important to be friendly?
    - What makes Wendell Friendly?
    - How are YOU friendly?
    - What does it mean to play fair?
    - Name some times when it's good to share.

TEACHER TIP

Have a stuffed teddy bear that kids can pass around as they talk.

Social Emotional

CARE TO BE FAIR
Shows Concern for Fairness

Activity 2
What Would Wendell Do?

Goal
Knowing that playing fair means sharing and taking turns.

- **Sit** the children in a circle around a table.
- **Deal Out** a specific number of jellybeans (an odd number for an even group; an even number for an odd group), counting out "one for you . . . one for me . . ." and then "two for you . . . two for me . . ." until all have been distributed.
- **Ask** each child to count the number in front of them. Let the children discover who has the extras and who has the shortages. Ask the children:
  - What would Wendell do?

MIND STRETCHERS

Budding Learners:
Be sure to dole out no more than five jellybeans each for budding learners. Let them count out loud as you point to each jellybean.

Blossoming Learners:
Dole out up to ten jellybeans for blossoming learners who can count higher. Can they count ALL the jellybeans on the table?

Social Emotional

CARE TO BE FAIR
Shows Concern for Fairness

- **Divide** the children into groups of three. Give each group two crayons and a cut-out shape of Friendly Wendell. Tell the children to color Wendell's face and body.

- As children discover there are not enough crayons for everyone, **encourage** them toward **taking turns** and **sharing** by asking:

    - What would Wendell do?

Social Emotional

CARE TO BE FAIR
Shows Concern for Fairness

Social Emotional

YOU CAN COUNT ON ME

Shows Responsibility

Activity 1
Read and discuss picture book *Strega Nona* by Tomie de Paolo

Goal
Understand responsibility

LET'S READ!

The Story of Strega Nona
by Tomie de Paolo

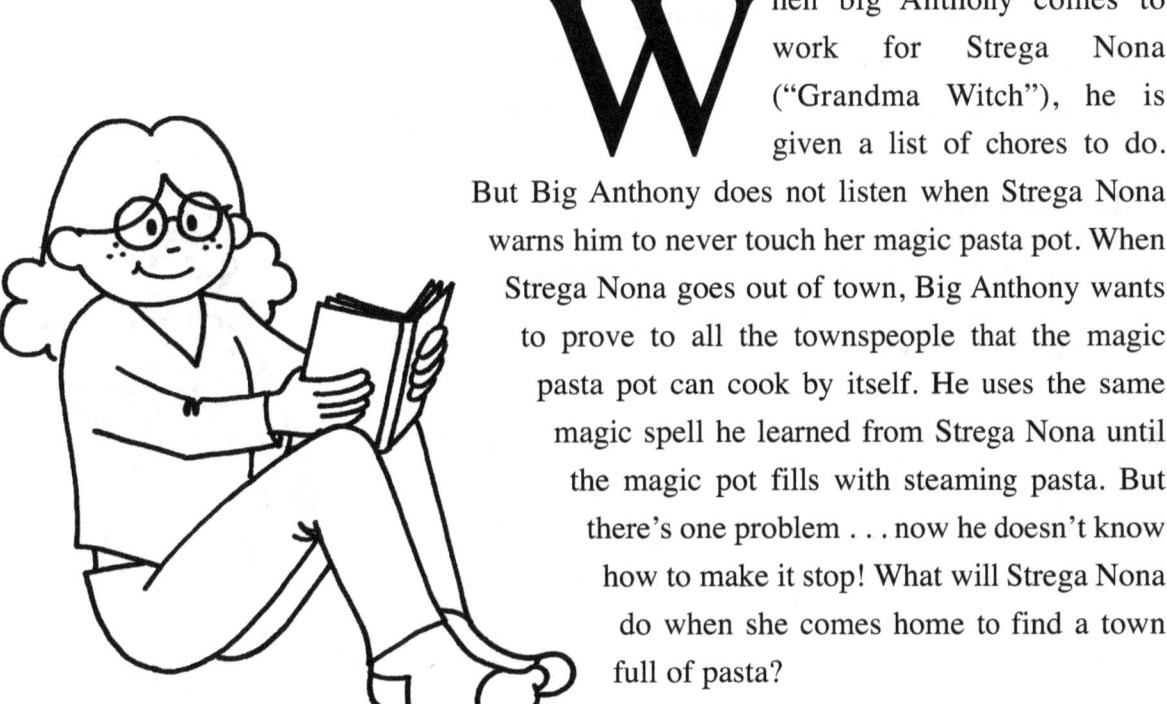

When big Anthony comes to work for Strega Nona ("Grandma Witch"), he is given a list of chores to do. But Big Anthony does not listen when Strega Nona warns him to never touch her magic pasta pot. When Strega Nona goes out of town, Big Anthony wants to prove to all the townspeople that the magic pasta pot can cook by itself. He uses the same magic spell he learned from Strega Nona until the magic pot fills with steaming pasta. But there's one problem . . . now he doesn't know how to make it stop! What will Strega Nona do when she comes home to find a town full of pasta?

Social Emotional

YOU CAN COUNT ON ME
Shows Responsibility

Activity 2
Play NONA SAYS!
(based on the classic game, *Simon Says*)

Goal
Stick to the rules of a game

LET'S PLAY NONA SAYS!

- The leader (Nona) asks players to gather around the "magic pot." (Use a plastic witch's cauldron, if available, or a regular pasta pot.)

- Nona gives instructions, but followers can only obey if the order is preceded by **"NONA SAYS."** If an instruction is **not** preceded by "NONA SAYS," then the player must step back from the group. Play continues until time limit is reached.

- **Sample Instructions:**
  - Nona says 'walk in a circle around the magic pot'
  - Nona says 'hop on one foot toward the magic pot'
  - Nona says 'walk backwards away from the magic pot'
  - Now touch your nose.

- After the game, talk about what it feels like to follow instructions. How does it feel when you forget? Do you think Big Anthony should practice playing **NONA SAYS** to help him remember to listen and pay attention?

Social Emotional

YOU CAN COUNT ON ME
Shows Responsibility

LET'S TALK!

- **About Responsibility . . .**
    - What does responsibility mean?
    - What are some different kinds of responsibilities?
    - Who do you count on in your life?

- **About the Story . . .**
    - How does Strega Nona show she is a caring person?
    - What are Big Anthony's responsibilities in the house?
    - Does Big Anthony show he is a responsible person when Strega None goes away?
    - Why do you think Big anthony doesn't listen to Strega Nona's instructions?
    - Do you think Big Anthony learns a lesson?
    - Do you think Big Anthony will be more responsible next time?
    - What can Big Anthony do to show Strega Nona that he is ready to be a better listener?

- **About You . . .**
    - Do you have chores . . . at home . . . at school?
    - How do you show that you are a responsible person?
    - What happens if you don't do your chores?
    - What other ways do you show you are responsible?

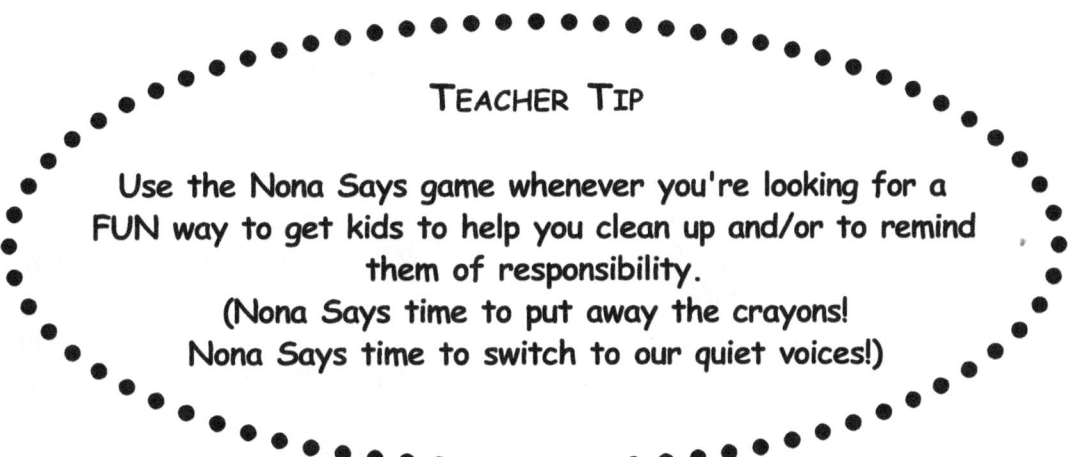

TEACHER TIP

Use the Nona Says game whenever you're looking for a FUN way to get kids to help you clean up and/or to remind them of responsibility.
(Nona Says time to put away the crayons!
Nona Says time to switch to our quiet voices!)

Social Emotional

YOU CAN COUNT ON ME
Shows Responsibility

Activity 3
Play RED LIGHT, GREEN LIGHT!

Goal
Improve listening

LET'S PLAY RED LIGHT, GREEN LIGHT!

Players try to touch the "traffic light" who, in turn, tries to avoid being touched.

- **Traffic light** stands 15 feet from the group, facing away from them. When **traffic light** says "green light!" all other players move toward him/her.

- At any time, **traffic light** can say "red light!" and turn around. If any of the players gets caught moving after "red light!" has been called, they are out.

- Play continues when **traffic light** turns back around and says "green light!"

- The **traffic light** wins if all players are out before anyone is able to touch him/her. Otherwise, the first player to touch the **traffic light** wins the game and becomes the **traffic light** for the next game.

MIND STRETCHERS

Budding Learners:
Teacher can assist by calling the light changes ("red light!...green light!") for budding-learner traffic lights. Traffic light turns around and back based on the teacher's calls.

Blossoming Learners:
No need for teacher assistance. Blossoming learner traffic lights can call their own light changes and turn around and back to "catch" the other players

Social Emotional

SHOULD I, SHOULDN'T I

Shows Awareness of Consequences

Activity 1
Play SHOULD I, SHOULDN'T I!

Goal
Understand there are consequences to most actions

My name is Waddle Happen! I often wonder ... Should I? ... or Shouldn't I? Maybe YOU can help me.

- Discuss all the possible **consequences** for the actions in the left column.

- Talk about **what could happen** to Waddle if he does each of these things.

- Help Waddle decide: **Should I?** or **Shouldn't I?**

Social Emotional

SHOULD I, SHOULDN'T I
Shows Awareness of Consequences

WHAT WILL HAPPEN IF I . . .	SHOULD I or SHOULDN'T I?
skate without my helmet	YES NO MAYBE
cover my mouth when I sneeze	YES NO MAYBE
dial 9-1-1 on the phone	YES NO MAYBE
throw a ball in the house	YES NO MAYBE
share my toys with friends	YES NO MAYBE
go near the stove	YES NO MAYBE
talk back to my mother/father	YES NO MAYBE

Social Emotional

SHOULD I, SHOULDN'T I
Shows Awareness of Consequences

Copy and cut out pictures of Waddle.
Make three vertical columns on a board: YES, NO, MAYBE

Social Emotional

SHOULD I, SHOULDN'T I
Shows Awareness of Consequences

Attach pictures under corresponding column
as children agree on YES, NO or MAYBE for each action.

Social Emotional

SHOULD I, SHOULDN'T I
Shows Awareness of Consequences

Social Emotional

SHOULD I, SHOULDN'T I
Shows Awareness of Consequences

MIND STRETCHERS

Budding Learners:

Budding learners may need more explanation with some examples (e.g., calling 9-1-1 may not <u>always</u> be the right thing to do.

Blossoming Learners:

Blossoming learners can tell if an action will trigger a good or bad consequence <u>and</u> can explain what the outcome will be.

Social Emotional

> ### EXPRESS IT OUT LOUD
> **Shows Creativity**
>
> **Activity 1**
> Read books to inspire creativity and imagination
>
> **Goal**
> Develop positive feelings about self-expression

LET'S READ!
Three great books to get the creative juices flowing . . .

Patrick McDonnell's **ART** shows young readers that "There's no stopping Art . . . when Art is inspired." A great book to inspire budding artists.

THE DOT and **ISH**, both by Peter Reynolds, are ideal for children who need a little extra encouragement. The book's lessons are simple and true: "Just make a mark and see where it takes you" . . . and . . . it's okay if your tree doesn't always look like a tree . . . a tree that looks tree-*ish* can be just as much fun! Try some "ish" art in the classroom to help free your little artists to express themselves!

Social Emotional

Express It Out Loud

Shows Creativity

Activity 2
Paint a Mural

Goal
Develop positive feelings about self-expression

Let's Paint!

- **Unroll** 5 - 6 feet of mural paper and tape it horizontally along a wall.

- **Encourage** children to "express themselves" by painting a mural.

- **Persuade** the young artists to look at the mural as many little masterpieces that can be viewed individually or all together as a combined "work of art."

Social Emotional

EXPRESS IT OUT LOUD
Shows Creativity

Activity 3
Create riddles and drawings with
ANIMAL CRACK-UPS or FRUIT LOOPIES theme.

Goal
Contribute original ideas and use imagination to be creative

ANIMAL CRACK-UPS!

What do you get when you cross a gorilla with an alligator?

A Gorillagator!

What other crazy animal combinations can you create?

snail + cheetah = sneetah

koala + elephant = koalaphant

flamingo + giraffe = flamaffe

kangaroo + rooster = kangarooster

Social Emotional

EXPRESS IT OUT LOUD
Shows Creativity

Now try it with fruit!

FRUIT LOOPIES!

What do you get when you cross a banana with an apple?

A Banapple!

What other loopy fruit combinations can you create?

plum + tangerine = plangerine

grape + cantaloupe = grantaloupe

cherry + mango = merrychango

raspberry + watermelon = raspermelon

Social Emotional

EXPRESS IT OUT LOUD
Shows Creativity

MIND STRETCHERS

Budding Learners:

If budding learners need help inventing their own riddle, name a pair for them, then let them come up with the punch line.

Blossoming Learners:

Are your blossoming learners on a roll? Encourage them to try writing a song about their Animal Crack-Up or Fruit Loopy!

Social Emotional

THE BEST ME I CAN BE

Shows Appropriate Values

Activity 1
Read and discuss *TEASING TROUBLE*
by Valerie Tripp

Goal
Show consideration for others

LET'S READ!

In Valerie Tripp's *TEASING TROUBLE*, Spencer loves to share jokes, but Hallie's not happy about being his punch line when he pokes fun at her loose teeth. The story is unique in that it appeals to two different points of view: Hallie learns you have to speak up to let someone know when their jokes are hurtful. Readers will review the "stand your ground" theme as well as the importance of showing consideration for others.

LET'S TALK!

- **About the Story . . .**
    - Why do you think Spencer likes to joke about Hallie's teeth?
    - Why does Hallie call Spencer a bully?
    - What does Hallie do to help Spencer understand that his jokes aren't very nice?

- **About YOU . . .**
    - Has anyone ever made a joke about you? How did it make you feel?
    - What's a good way to let people known when a joke makes you sad?
    - Have you ever made jokes about other people? Did it make them laugh or hurt their feelings?
    - What can you do to make sure your jokes are nice for everyone?
    - What's the difference between a joke and teasing?

Social Emotional

THE BEST ME I CAN BE
Shows Appropriate Values

MIND STRETCHERS

Budding Learners:

Give examples of jokes that are funny and jokes that are hurtful. Ask budding learners to respond with "funny" or "not nice."

Blossoming Learners:

Ask "What's the best me I can be?" Look for answers like sense of humor, consideration, standing my ground, self control . . .

Social Emotional

THE BEST ME I CAN BE

Shows Appropriate Values

Activity 2
Play QUIET MEETING

Goal
Share a sense of humor and demonstrate self-discipline

LET'S PLAY!

- One player is the "Meeting Manager" (MM). The MM sits facing the other players.
- When ready, the MM recites the verse:

  Quiet Meeting has begun
  No more laughing, mo more fun.
  If you dare to crack a smile,
  You may have to walk a mile.

- After reciting the verse, the MM begins to make funny faces or noises, tell jokes, dance, or do just about anything (except touch another player) to try to get someone to laugh.

- The first person to laugh must "walk a mile" (i.e., walk around the room, around the group of players, or whatever is decided) and then take his/her place in front of the players as the new MM.

- Play continues - with the new MM trying to get other players to smile or laugh - as long as time allots, or until everyone has had a turn to be Meeting Manager.

Social Emotional

THE BEST ME I CAN BE
Shows Appropriate Values

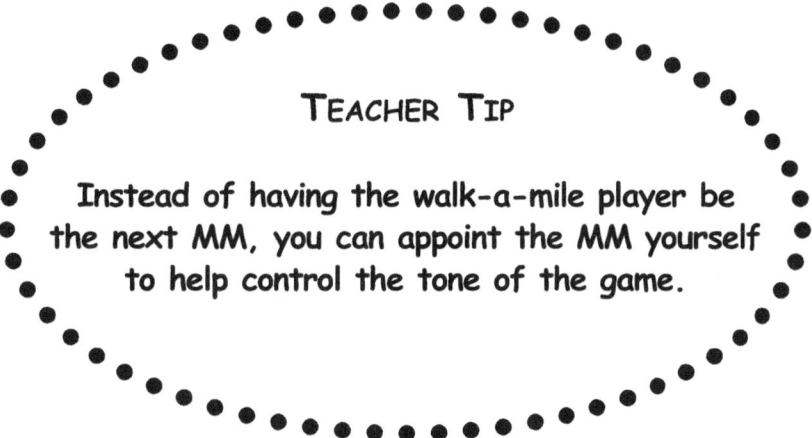

TEACHER TIP

Instead of having the walk-a-mile player be the next MM, you can appoint the MM yourself to help control the tone of the game.

LET'S TALK!

- How does it feel when someone makes you laugh?

- What does it take to get someone to laugh? Is it important to know something about that person?

- What is a sense of humor? What makes you laugh the most?

- Why is it good to have a sense of humor? . . . about yourself? . . . about others? . . . about situations?

- When is the right time for jokes and laughing? When is the wrong time? (re-emphasize the importance of not joking or laughing at the expense of others.)

- Were you able to hold your laughter inside?

- What does it feel like to keep from laughing at a joke or a silly act?

- What does it take to control a laugh?

Social Emotional

FINDING FRIENDS
Makes Friends

Activity 1
Read and discuss picture book *BEING FRIENDS* by Karen Beaumont

Goal
Discover that different personalities can make great friends

LET'S READ!

In *BEING FRIENDS*, by Karen Beaumont, readers follow the best friendship of two amusing little girls who share a very strong bond in spite of and because of their many differences.

LET'S TALK!

● **About the Story . . .**

- What makes the two friends so different?
- What do the friends have in common?
- Why do you think they are best friends?

● **About YOU . . .**

- Think about your best friend. Where/how did you meet?
- In what ways are you different? In what ways are you the same?
- What new things have you learned from your best friend?
- What has your best friend learned from you?

Social Emotional

FINDING FRIENDS
Makes Friends

Activity 2
Find new friends

Goal
Discover that learning about others can lead to new friendships

LET'S SHARE!

- **GATHER** children in a circle on the floor. Move around the circle asking each child in turn to name two things about themselves they'd like to share (e.g., favorite food and favorite color).

- After a child has named his/her two things, have the other children **REPEAT** the answers back (e.g., "Samantha's favorite food is _____ . . . and Samantha's favorite color is _____.") Then move on to the next child in the circle.

- When everyone has had a turn, go around the circle **ONE MORE TIME**. This time, each child has a turn to stay silent as the others volunteer to tell the two things they've learned about him/her. The child being discussed can chime in with hints if necessary.

- After the exercise, **TALK ABOUT** why it's fun/important to learn new things about people, and why it's also fun to have a turn to tell about yourself. How does this help build friendships?

Social Emotional

FINDING FRIENDS
Makes Friends

Activity 3
Make a BUDDY SQUARE

Goal
Practice partnership and teamwork with a friend

LET'S BUDDY UP!

- Have children **PAIR UP** with a buddy. Give each pair one square sheet of drawing paper and some crayons or markers.

- Help each pair to **FOLD THEIR PAPER** in half diagonally with a crease down the middle. Tell them that each person in the pair will be designing one side of the paper.

- Ask all the buddy #1's to **MAKE A SQUIGGLE** in their favorite color. Then have the pair turn the paper over and have buddy #2 do the same on his/her side. Then ask buddy #1 to **DRAW** his/her favorite animal. Next, turn the paper over the buddy #2 does the same . . . and so on with other fun things to draw until the page is filled.

- When finished, tell each buddy pair to **UNFOLD** their papers to reveal their beautiful buddy squares.

- **WRITE** the children's names on the squares and display them for all to see.

Buddy Square example

Social Emotional

FINDING FRIENDS
Makes Friends

MIND STRETCHERS

Budding Learners:

Encourage partnership between timid budding learners by pointing out likenesses on their square while they're still drawing.

Blossoming Learners:

If blossoming learners feel comfortable doing so, encourage them to present their BUDDY SQUARE to the group.

Social Emotional

THE MANY COLORS OF ME
Shows Varying Emotions

Activity 1
Read and discuss
Dr. Seuss's *MY MANY COLORED DAYS*
and Jamie Lee Curtis's *TODAY I FEEL SILLY*

Goal
Explore a variety of different emotions

LET'S READ!
Two books for exploring moods and feelings

Dr. Seuss's *MY MANY COLORED DAYS* is an enduring classic that helps young readers explore their moods through the many colors of the rainbow.

TODAY I FEEL SILLY & *Other Moods That Make My Day*, by Jamie Lee Curtis, follows a little girl through 13 different types of feelings and teaches that swinging through moods is a-okay.

TEACHER TIP

Review the colors of the RAINBOW and talk about how rain + sun (two different moods) can produce such a beautiful effect.

Social Emotional

THE MANY COLORS OF ME
Shows Varying Emotions

LET'S TALK!

- Review the colors of the rainbow. Talk about warm colors, cool colors, hot colors and cold colors.

- What color do you feel when you're happy? . . . angry? . . . sad? . . . excited? . . . confused? . . . sick? . . . eager? . . . hungry? . . . cold? . . . warm?

- Do you ever feel more than one color on the same day? . . . at the same time?

- Besides colors, what are other ways to express our moods? (facial expressions, giggles, cartwheels, dragging feet, crying, hugging . . .)

MIND STRETCHERS

Budding Learners:

Help budding learners express their moods by copying your facial expressions and gestures. Have fun with it!

Blossoming Learners:

Encourage blossoming learners to describe their moods with words. Remind them that many moods in one day is a-okay.

Social Emotional

THE MANY COLORS OF ME
Shows Varying Emotions

Activity 2
Make a MANY COLORS OF ME door hanger buddy

Goal
Understand that one person has many moods/colors

- **COPY** the door hanger pattern on the opposite page. **CUT** out the pattern and trace it onto a sheet of white fun foam (available in craft stores). Then **CUT** the shape out of the foam. **GIVE** one to each child.

- **INVITE** children to color their door hanger buddies with all the colors they feel inside them.

- **TELL** children to bring their buddies home to hand on their bedroom doors to remind their families (and themselves) that they have a rainbow of colors inside them.

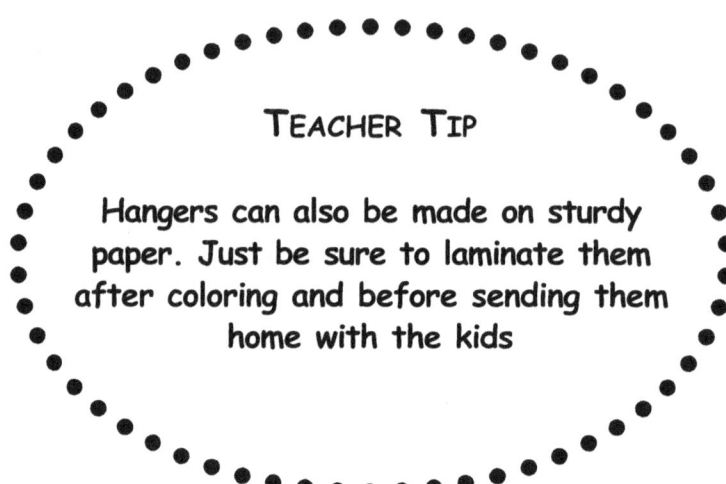

TEACHER TIP

Hangers can also be made on sturdy paper. Just be sure to laminate them after coloring and before sending them home with the kids

Social Emotional

THE MANY COLORS OF ME
Shows Varying Emotions

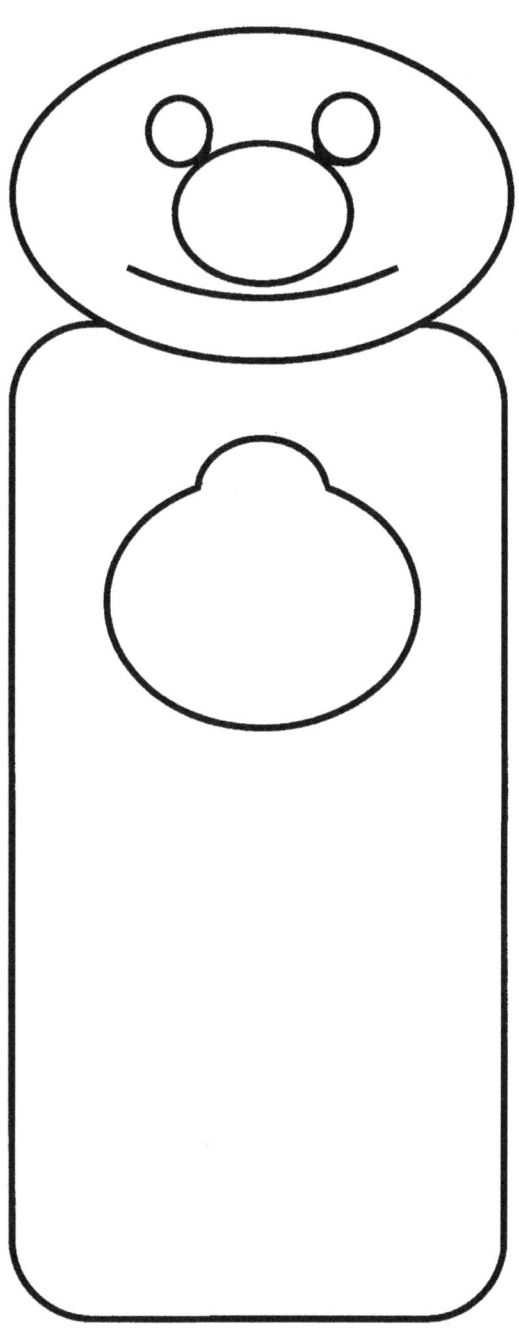

Social Emotional

THE MANY COLORS OF ME
Shows Varying Emotions

Colors aren't the only way to express feelings. Turning a pumpkin into a Jack O'Lantern is a great way for a child to see and learn all that a facial expression can convey.

Make the Jack O'Lanterns . . . and then talk about what their faces are "saying."

Social Emotional

THE MANY COLORS OF ME
Shows Varying Emotions

Activity 3
Make JACK O'LANTERN faces

Goal
Show feelings with colors and facial expressions

- **COPY** the Jack O'Lantern pieces on the following page and give a full set to each child. Let them cut out the pieces. (Some may need help with scissors).

- **ENCOURAGE** children to color their pumpkins with whatever color they "fee like" today.

- Next **INVITE** them to paste on the features that show the Jack O'Lantern face they want to show today.

TEACHER TIP

Why not save this activity for Halloween time and use the real thing?

Buy some mini pumpkins from your local grocery store or pumpkin patch. then give the kids some peel-off face features stickers (or use colored paint markers) to decorate our pumpkin faces.

Social Emotional

THE MANY COLORS OF ME
Shows Varying Emotions

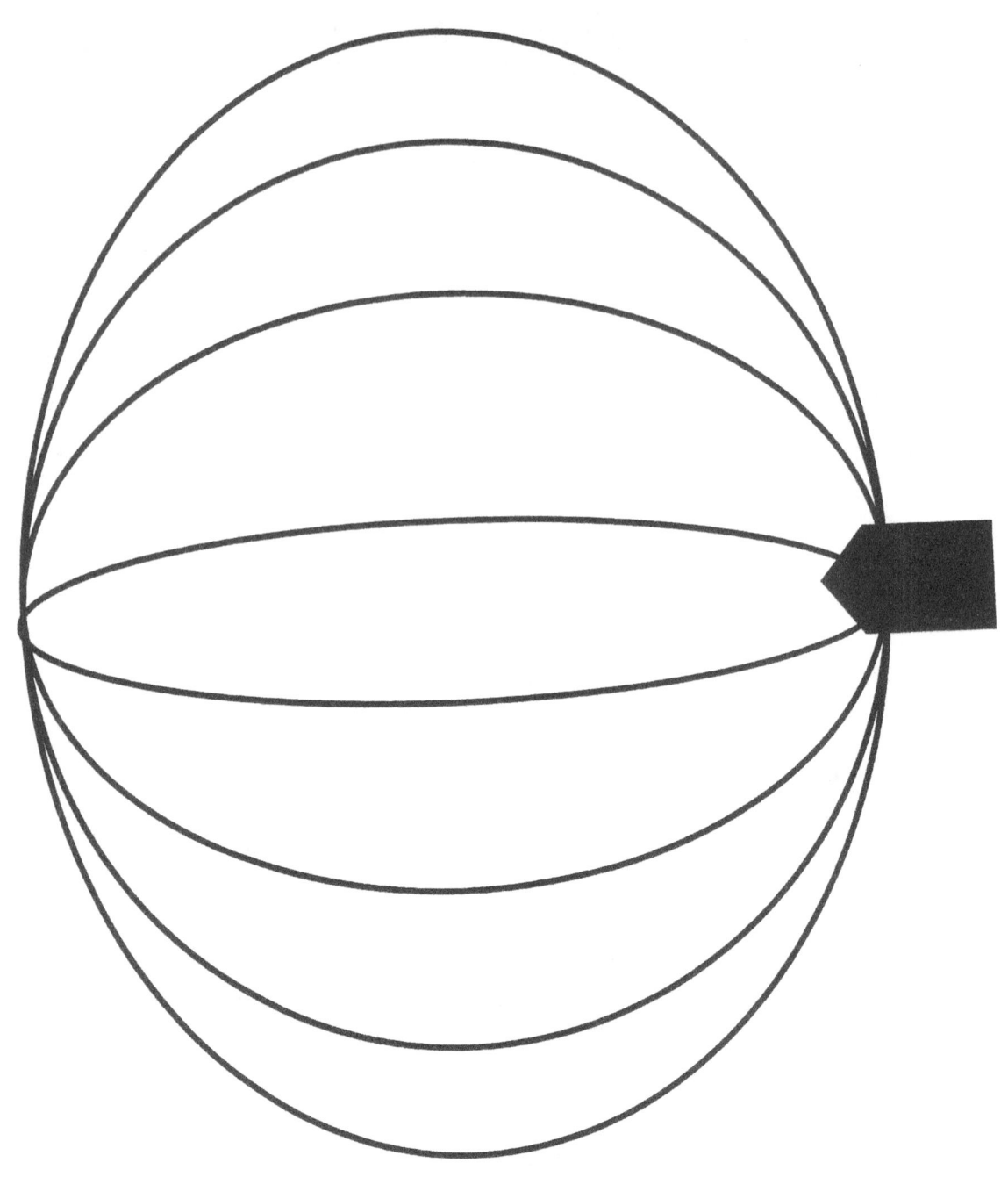

Social Emotional

THE MANY COLORS OF ME
Shows Varying Emotions

Language

UNIT 2
Developmental Activities

Do Tell
Sequences and retells

Picture This
Shows reading interest

Reader Ready
Knows reading progression

Now I Know My ABC's
Knows alphabet

Out Of My Head
Uses imagination

If I Were You
Plays roles

Knock, Knock, Tick, Tock
Discriminates consonants

You Can Say That Again
Speaks informally

Language

Do Tell
Sequences and Retells

MY PICNIC BOX

I opened up my picnic box and who popped out?
ONE BABY ELEPHANT, round and stout.

I opened up my picnic box and who came to play?
TWO BABY KITTY CATS, soft and gray.

I opened up my picnic box and out there flew
THREE BABY BUTTERFLIES, yellow, pink, and blue.

I opened up my picnic box and who was there?
FOUR BABY BUMBLEBEES buzzing in the air.

I opened up my picnic box and who came to call?
FIVE BABY PICNIC ANTS, hungry and small.

Then those **FIVE BABY PICNIC ANTS**,
hungry and small,
nibbled on my sandwich and . . .

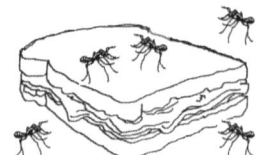

    ate . . . it . . . all!

54

Language

DO TELL
Sequences and Retells

Activity 1
Retell the *MY PICNIC BOX* story

Goal
Retell a simple story in the proper order

LET'S READ & TALK!

- **READ** *MY PICNIC BOX* aloud two times.

- **ASK** for answers to the following questions:

    - **Who was in the picnic box?** (Take note of how many creatures kids can remember. Don't be concerned at this point that they know how many of each there are.

    - **How many elephants are in the picnic box?**

    - **Who is soft and gray?**

    - **Who is yellow, pink and blue?**

    - **What do the bumblebees do?**

    - **Who is small and hungry?**

    - **What do the baby picnic ants do?**

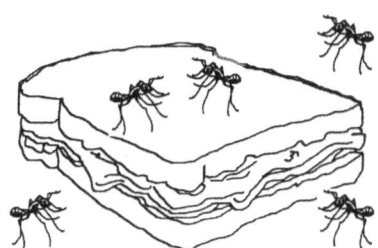

55

Language

> **DO TELL**
>
> **Sequences and Retells**
>
> **Activity 2**
> Match the Numbers
>
> **Goal**
> Recognize number values

- **CUT OUT** the picture and number flash cards on the following pages.

- **ASK** the children to match the number flash cards with the picture flash card that has the same number of items.

Language

DO TELL
Sequences and Retells

Language

DO TELL
Sequences and Retells

1	2	3
4	5	6

Language

PICTURE THIS
Shows Reading Interest

Activity 1
Share the Fruit Fun Read-Along

Goal
Develop left-to-right eye movement in preparation for reading

LET'S READ!

- **Let** child "read" the pictures as the story goes along.
- **Use** your finger to keep the place in the story.
- **Encourage** children to fill in the missing words.

 FRUIT FUN!

One day, a little 👧 and a little 👦 went to a 🏪. It was filled with all kinds of 🍎. There were 🍎 and 🍌 and 🍒 and 🥥.

"Mom says we should eat lots of 🍎," said the little 👧. "Let's buy some 🍎.

"I don't like 🍎," said the little 👦. "I like 🍋."
"

Language

PICTURE THIS
Shows Reading Interest

But I don't like 🥥," said the little 👧. "Let's pick something we both like," said the little 👦. "We both like 🍌 and we both like 🍒."

"Okay," said the little 👧. And they loaded the 🍌 and 🍒 into the 🛒.

"I have another idea," said the little 👦. "I'll be right back." Then he took the 🛒 to another side of the 🏪.

When they got 🏠 the little 👧 and the little 👦 opened the 🛍️🛍️. The little 👦 found the 🍌 and the 🍒 in one 🛍️. In the other 🛍️ the little 👧 found a big surprise! There was some 🍦, and a bottle of chocolate 🍫.

60

Language

PICTURE THIS
Shows Reading Interest

"What's all this?" asked the little 👧.

"I'll show you," said the little 👦.

He sliced the 🍌 and put them in a bowl. Then he put two scoops of 🍦 on top of the 🍌. He poured the 🍫 on top of the 🍦. He topped it all off with the fresh 🍒.

"You see," said the little 👦. "This is how I like to eat my 🍨!"

"Me too!" said the little 👧.

And together they enjoyed a delicious 🍨!

Language

PICTURE THIS
Shows Reading Interest

Activity 2
Read *THE RED BOOK* by Barbara Lehman
and *GOOD DOG, CARL* by Alexandra Day

Goal
Develop confidence with independent "reading"

LET'S READ!
Two books for pre-readers to enjoy by themselves...

Barbara Lehman's *THE RED BOOK* describes itself as a "magical red book without any words" that takes us on an adventure "through the power of story."

In *GOOD DOG, CARL* (and the other books in the *GOOD DOG* series), Alexandra Day tells the story by showing (through pictures only) the non-stop activities of a busy rottweiler named Carl.

MIND STRETCHERS

Budding Learners:

Pictures-only story books are a great way for budding learners to try "reading" aloud. Let them turn the pages and tell you the story.

Blossoming Learners:

Blossoming learners can enjoy "reading" time all by themselves as they page through a picture story book unassisted.

Language

READER READY
Knows Reading Progression

Activity 1
MATT THE RACER MAZE

Goal
Use left-to-right eye movement to develop reading progression skills

Help Matt the Racer get to the finish line to win his trophy!
(Continue to build this skill by providing other mazed like this one.)

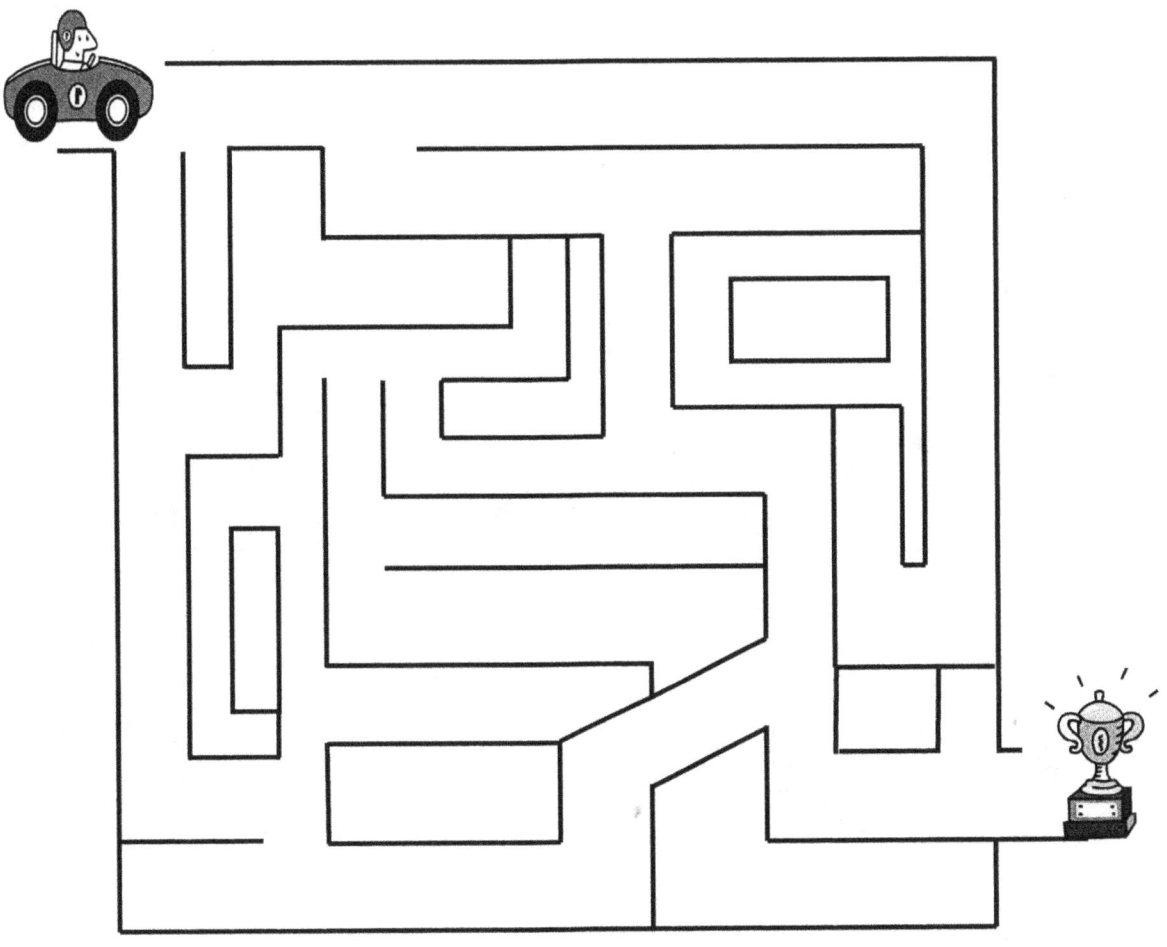

Language

READER READY
Knows Reading Progression

Activity 2
ANIMAL MATCH-UPS & OBJECT LOOK-ALIKES

Goal
Use up-down and left-to-right eye movement to develop reading progression skills and identify likes and differences

ON THE FOLLOWING PAGES . . .

- In **ANIMAL MATCH-UPS, ASSIST** child in using a pencil to follow the lines from the animal on the left to the object on the right.

- In **LOOK-ALIKES, ASK** child to find the picture that looks the same as the picture in the box at left.

- **CONTINUE** building this skill through other up-down/left-to-right match-up activities like these.

MIND STRETCHERS

Budding Learners:

Budding learners may need help drawing along or within the lines. Activities like **Animal Match-Ups** are good pencil practice!

Blossoming Learners:

After blossoming learners find the matches in the **Look-Alike** activity, next ask them to tell HOW the objects are alike . . . or different..

Language

READER READY
Knows Reading Progression

ANIMAL MATCH-UP
Use a pencil to follow the lines from object on left to object on right.

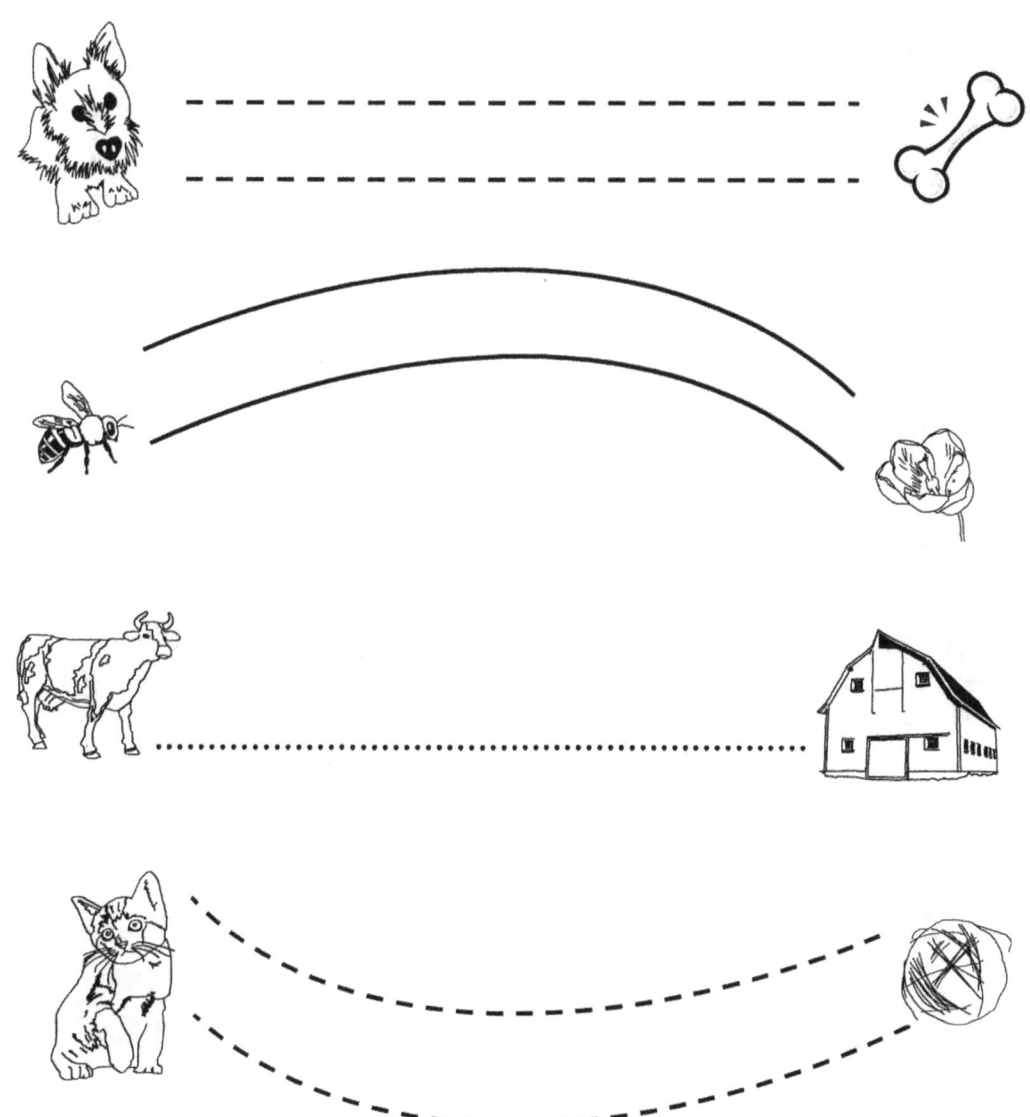

Language

> **READER READY**
> Knows Reading Progression

OBJECT LOOK-ALIKES
Find the picture that looks the same as the picture in the box at left.

Language

NOW I KNOW MY ABC'S

Knows Alphabet

Activity 1
Fun with ABC Critters

Goal
Know and name the letters of the alphabet.

- **COPY** and **PASTE** each ABC verse onto a separate flash card. Have children point to all the A's in the A verse, all the B's in the B verse, and so on.

- Next, ask child to trace (with finger) the highlighted letters at the bottom of each card.

Alvin the **a**nt
h**a**s **a** pet **a**ntelope
who **ea**ts nothing but **a**pples
and fresh c**a**nt**a**loupe.

Aa

Bobby the **b**ear
bit a **b**erry or two.
You can tell **b**ecause now
Bobby's tongue is all **b**lue.

Bb

Language

NOW I KNOW MY ABC'S
Knows Alphabet

Carlos the **c**lam
played a **c**larinet tune.
All the **c**rabs **c**licked their **c**laws
as they dan**c**ed by the moon.

Cc

Demetri the **d**onkey
did not **d**o his chores,
so his **d**ad told **D**emetri
he must stay in**d**oors.

Dd

Ella the **ele**phant
would w**e**ar a wig
exc**e**pt **E**lla discov**e**r**e**d
h**e**r **e**ars ar**e** too big.

Ee

Language

NOW I KNOW MY ABC'S
Knows Alphabet

Fancy **F**inola,
the **f**riendly gray **f**ox,
likes to **f**rolic all day
in her **f**lu**ff**y green socks.

Ff

Gary the **g**roundho**g**
gets **g**ood friends to**g**ether
for **g**ames, and to **g**ossip
about the day's weather.

Gg

Have you **h**eard about **H**ilda,
t**h**e **h**og from the mill?
Hilda dances the **h**ula
eac**h** day on the **h**ill.

Hh

Language

NOW I KNOW MY ABC'S
Knows Alphabet

Izzie the **i**nchworm
left **i**nk **i**n the s**i**nk.
I can tell because **I**zzie
has p**i**nk **i**nk . . . **I** think!

Ii

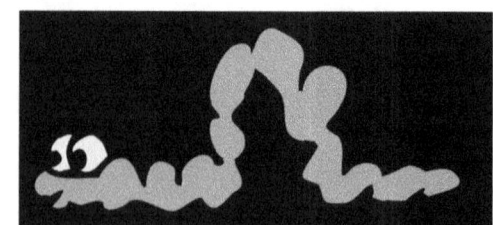

Jojo the **j**ellyfish
jiggles and **j**iggles.
Just tell a good **j**oke,
and she giggles and giggles.

Jj

Kangaroo **K**al
lost his **k**ite in **K**entucky.
He found it again
the next day. **K**al was luc**k**y.

Kk

Language

NOW I KNOW MY ABC'S
Knows Alphabet

Lo**l**a the **l**eopard
likes **l**icorice whips.
Lo**l**a s**l**urps them in s**l**owly
then **l**icks up her **l**ips.

Ll

Monica **m**ole
has e**m**erged fro**m** her hole.
After all, this is **M**onday . . .
It's ti**m**e to go bowl.

Mm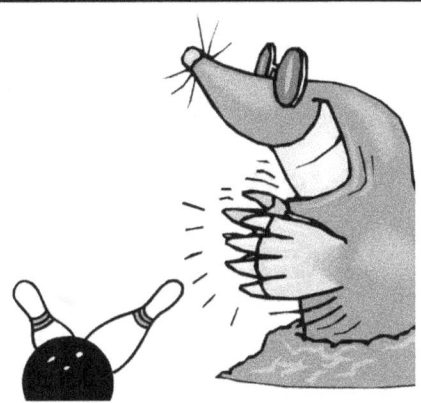

Old **n**an**n**y goat **N**i**n**a
ca**n n**ever remember
her birthday, which rolls arou**n**d
every **N**ovember.

Nn

Language

NOW I KNOW MY ABC'S
Knows Alphabet

Oscar the **o**strich
sang **o**pera f**o**r years
while his r**oo**mmate, **O**thell**o**
sh**o**ved s**o**cks in his ears.

Oo

Penelo**p**e **p**enguin
makes **p**op**c**orn for **P**aul.
He's the **p**lum**p** little **p**enguin
who lives down the hall.

Pp

Quimby is **q**uite
a uni**q**ue little **q**uail.
He delivers our mail
every day without fail.

Qq

Language

NOW I KNOW MY ABC's
Knows Alphabet

Robert the **r**at
makes **r**ed **r**aspbe**rr**y sauce
which he sha**r**es with his
rodent f**r**iends, **R**iley and **R**oss.

Rr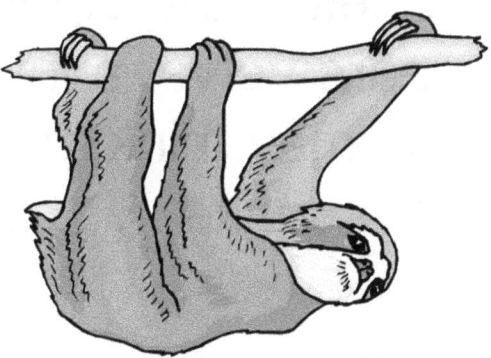

Sonny**'s** a **s**loth
You might **s**ay he **is** boring.
He **s**pend**s s**o much time
sound a**s**leep, **s**imply **s**noring.

Ss

This **t**iger named **T**errence
will **t**oot his **t**rombone
'til his **t**u**t**or can **t**each him
to play saxophone.

Tt

Language

NOW I KNOW MY ABC'S
Knows Alphabet

Urs**u**la **u**rchin
lives **u**nder the sea.
She feels sn**u**g **u**nder there.
Will she come **u**p? We'll see.

Uu

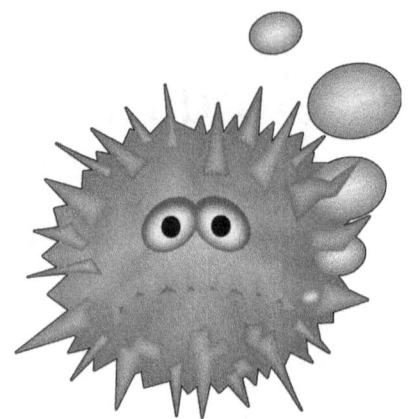

Vanessa the **v**iper
wears **v**el**v**et a lot.
You may think that is odd
for a snake . . . but it's not.

Vv

Willy the **w**allaby
waltzed for a while
but he s**w**itched to a tango.
It's much more his style.

Ww

Language

NOW I KNOW MY ABC's
Knows Alphabet

Xavier the lyn**x**
is e**x**cited to tell
he can play his new **x**ylophone
e**x**pertly well.

Xx

Yolanda the **y**ak
wears a **y**ellow backpack.
Ever**y** da**y** she packs cra**y**ons,
a book, and a snack.

Yy

A **z**ebra named **z**ero
sowed seeds that were teeny.
They grew into do**z**ens of
da**zz**ling **z**ucchini.

Zz

Language

NOW I KNOW MY ABC'S

Knows Alphabet

Activity 2
How many **B**'s in the honeycomb?

Goal
Recognize uppercase and lowercase **B**'s.

Help Mrs. Bree, the bumblebee find all the B's in her honeycomb.

- **USE** a **YELLOW CRAYON** to color all the honeycombs with **B** or **b**.

- **COLOR** the rest of the honeycomb in your favorite colors.

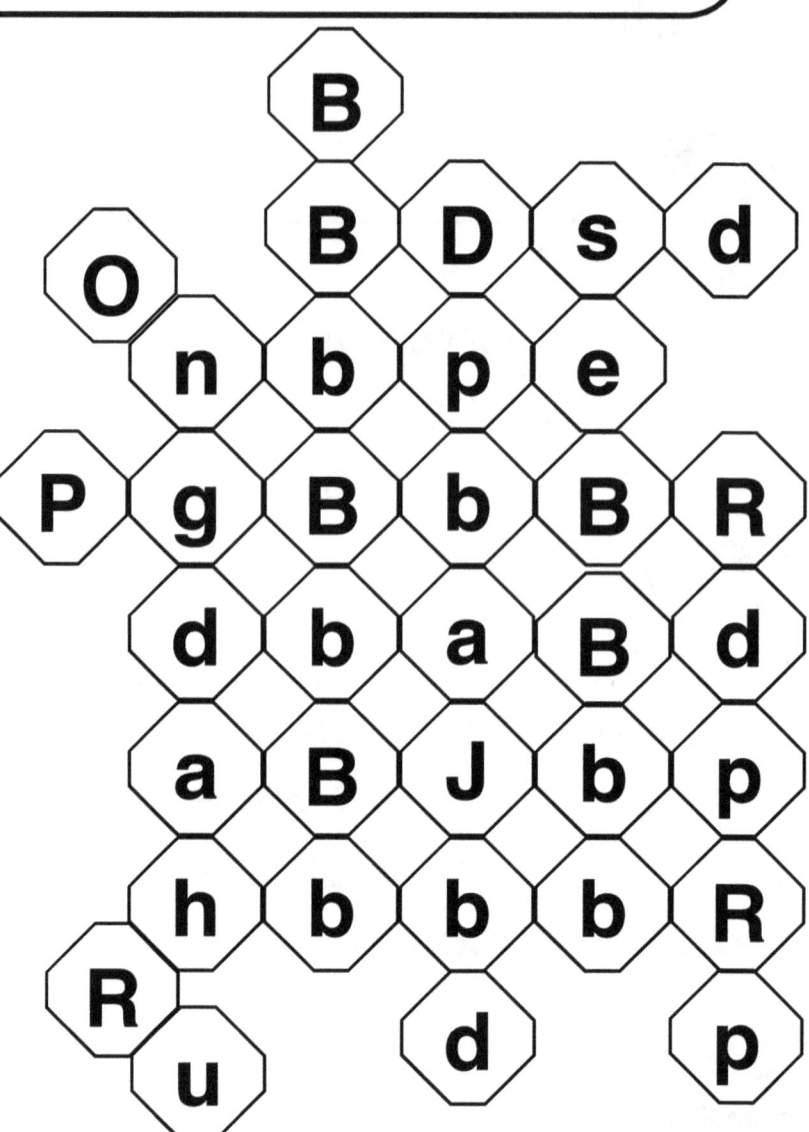

Language

NOW I KNOW MY ABC'S
Knows Alphabet

TEACHER TIP

Make Activity 2 more challenging by giving more color-coding instructions. (Example: Color all B's yellow; color all other uppercase letters orange; color all other lowercase letter red . . .) See if kids can discover the hidden letter that emerges in yellow.

Language

NOW I KNOW MY ABC'S

Knows Alphabet

Activity 3
Mrs. Bree the Bumblebee

Goal
Practice writing and "reading progressions."

Mrs. Bree, the bumblebee, is going to the store. What does Mrs. Bree tell her baby bee before buzzing out the door?

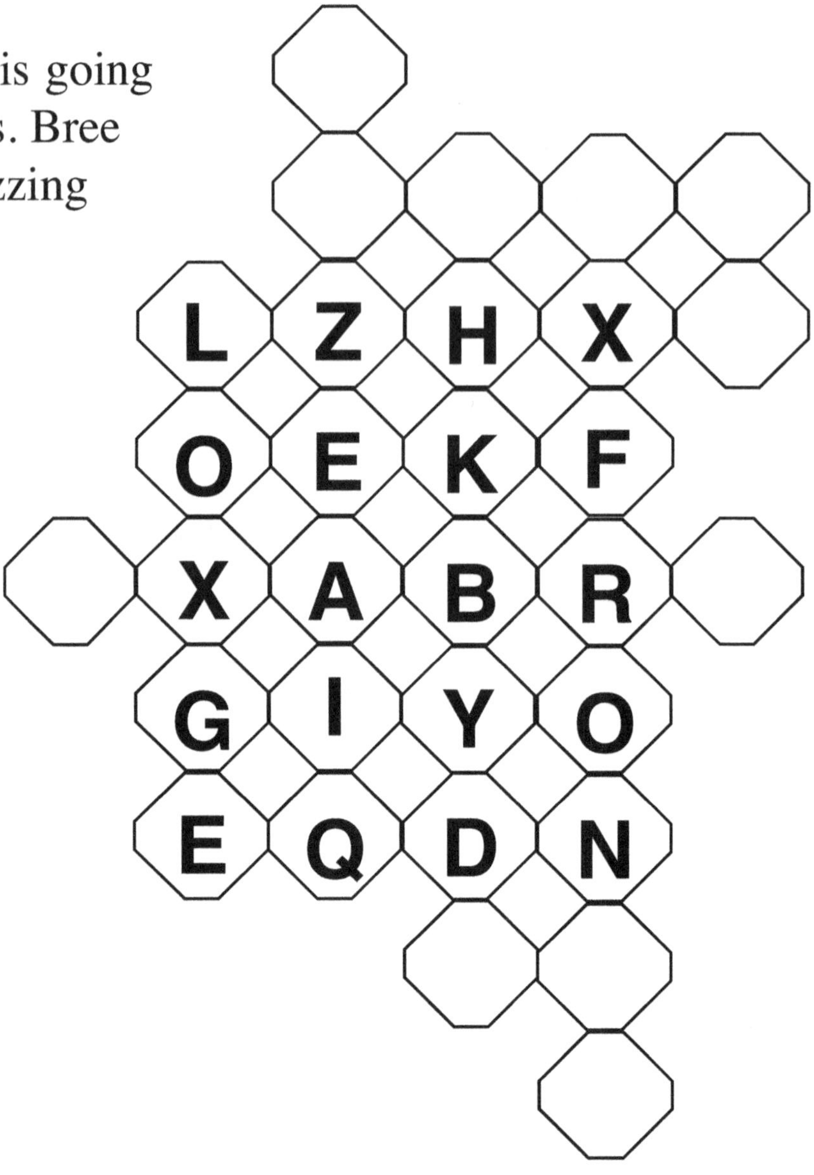

FIND THE LETTER THAT IS...

below K and between A and R _____

next to Q and below G _____

above A and below Z _____

below X and next to I _____

next to Y and between R and N _____

above X and below L _____

between Q and N and below Y _____

78

Language

NOW I KNOW MY ABC'S
Knows Alphabet

MIND STRETCHERS

Budding Learners:

Budding learners can search for all the **B**'s in the honeycomb in **Activity 2**.

Blossoming Learners:

Blossoming learners can solve the bumblebee puzzle in **Activity 3**.

Language

OUT OF MY HEAD
Uses Imagination

Activity 1
Build a Story

Goal
Build a funny story based on a familiar rhyme

LET'S BUILD A STORY!

- **INVITE** children to contribute **building block words** to help build the story on the next page. Don't reveal the rest of the story until AFTER they've contributed their **building block words** based on the clues you give them.

- **TELL** children they are using their **IMAGINATIONS** to re-tell a familiar story. The result will be their very own made-up funny story!

- After filling in all the blanks, **READ ALOUD** the complete story with the kids' original words plugged in.

- **CELEBRATE** the humor and originality of the story they built together.● Talk about what it means to **USE YOUR IMAGINATION!**

Language

OUT OF MY HEAD
Uses Imagination

THE STORY OF _____ & JILL
[name]

_____ and Jill
[name from title above]

went up a hill to fetch a _____
[container]

of _____.
[liquid]

_____ fell down
[name from title above]

and broke his/her) _____ and Jill
[body part]

shouted _____!!!
[something to yell/scream/cry out]

TEACHER TIP

Try this same activity with other familiar nursery rhymes, fairy tales, short stories, or songs.

Language

OUT OF MY HEAD
Uses Imagination

Activity 2
Play a game of "AND THEN . . ." to create a story

Goal
Use imagination to create a simple story with logical sequence

LET'S IMAGINE!

- **GATHER** children for a **story circle**. **INVITE** them to open their imaginations. We're going to create our very own group story . . . one simple sentence at a time. (Instead of giving building block words, this time we'll be making **building block sentences**.)

- **BEGIN** the story by contributing the first simple sentence. **END** your turn by saying the words **AND THEN . . .** and instruct children to do the same. Each child in turn will contribute one simple sentence that builds on the idea introduced in the previous sentence. The child then says **"AND THEN. . ."** as a pass-off to the next story-teller.

EXAMPLE:

Teacher: *One morning, I woke up with a purple frog in my nose.* **And then. . .**

Storyteller 1: *I said, "Hello, purple frog,"* **And then. . .**

Storyteller 2: *The frog croaked at me.* **And then. . .**

Storyteller 3: *My mother came into my room.* **And then. . .**

Storyteller 4: *The purple frog hopped down to the floor. And then. . .*

Storyteller 5: *The frog ran out of my bedroom and down the hall.* **And then. . .**

Language

OUT OF MY HEAD
Uses Imagination

Activity 3
Make your own picture book

Goal
Create pictures to illustrate the new story

LET'S ADD PICTURES!

- **SHOW** children 2-3 familiar classroom picture books.

- **EXPLAIN** the role of the illustrator. (Tell children that every picture book story has a writer and an illustrator, or artist. Sometimes the writer and illustrator are the same person. Example: Maurice Sendak, *WHERE THE WILD THINGS ARE*.)

- **ASK** children for help in creating a title for the story they created as a group (e.g., The Purple Frog.)

- **HAND OUT** one sheet of paper to each child along with crayons, markers or colored pencils. **ASK** each child to draw a picture that represents his sentence in the story (e.g., "The frog croaked at me.")

- **ASK** children to help you **ARRANGE** all the pictures in the proper sequence to tell the story. Then **FASTEN** the pages (using three-hole-punch and binder clips or fasteners.)

- **GATHER** children back to the circle for story time and **READ** them the new picture book that **they** created!

Language

OUT OF MY HEAD
Uses Imagination

TEACHER TIP

The Out Of My Head Activity 3 (on previous page) involves group collaboration on one picture book, which can then be shared with the entire class.

Another option for this activity is to provide each child with a small stack of index cards (one for each sentence from the story) and ask them to draw a picture to represent each sentence. Then punch one hole in each of the top left corners of the index cards and bind them with a small binder ring. Now each child has his/her own picture flip-book!

MIND STRETCHERS

Budding Learners:

Budding learners should be encouraged to re-tell their picture book story to their family.

Blossoming Learners:

Blossoming learners may want to try "reading" the picture book to the rest of the class. Ask for volunteers!

Language

IF I WERE YOU

Plays Roles

Activity 1
Role Play at the FINER DINER

Goal
Play the everyday roles of diner workers and customers

LET'S PLAY!

- **ASSIGN** roles for children to play at the finer diner! (Number of roles can be adjusted based on class size and role interest. There are no limits on roles other than making sure there's at least one customer, one server and one chef.

- **ENCOURAGE** kids to make up their own character names if they prefer!

GIRL ROLES	BOY ROLES
Chef Shelly	Chef Jeff
Chef Sheila	Chef Sheldon
Chef Sherry	Chef Shawn

Server Sara	Server Sal
Server Sandy	Server Sam
Server Sissy	Server Stanley

Customer Carla	Customer Connor
Customer Kelly	Customer Colby
Customer Cora	Customer Calvin
Customer Kate	Customer Clinton
Customer Kim	Customer Kenny

Language

IF I WERE YOU
Plays Roles

- **USE** the templates below to create **FINER DINER** name tags for each child participating in the role play. Children can use a character name from the list on the previous page or use their own names (either real or made-up).

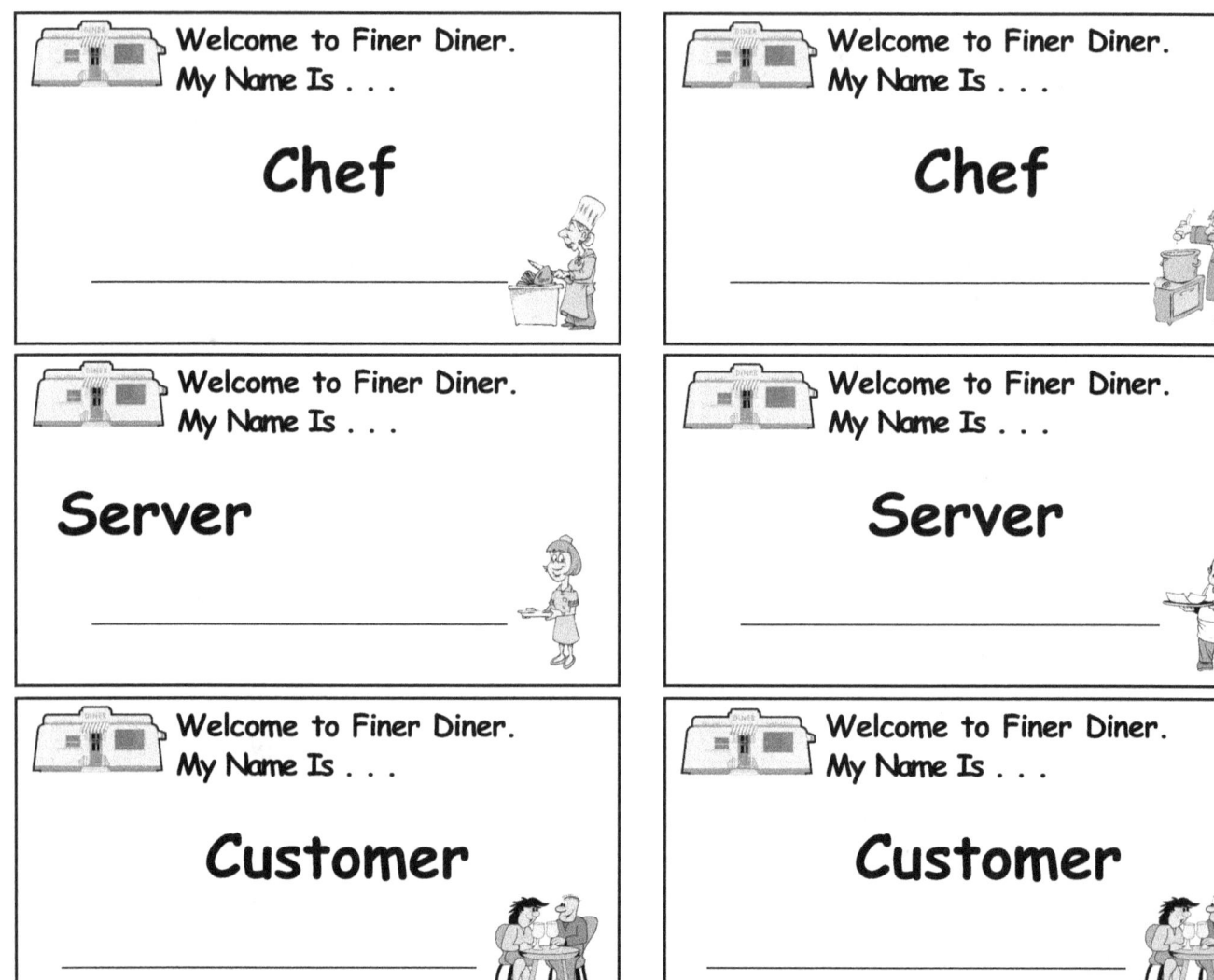

- **COPY** the next two pages for **FINER DINER** menus and order forms.

Language

IF I WERE YOU
Plays Roles

FINER DINER MENU

Main Dishes

Side Dishes

Desserts

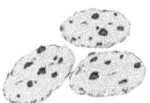    

Language

IF I WERE YOU
Plays Roles

FINER DINER FOOD ORDER

Language

IF I WERE YOU
Plays Roles

- **USE** the template below to make **FINER DINER** money.

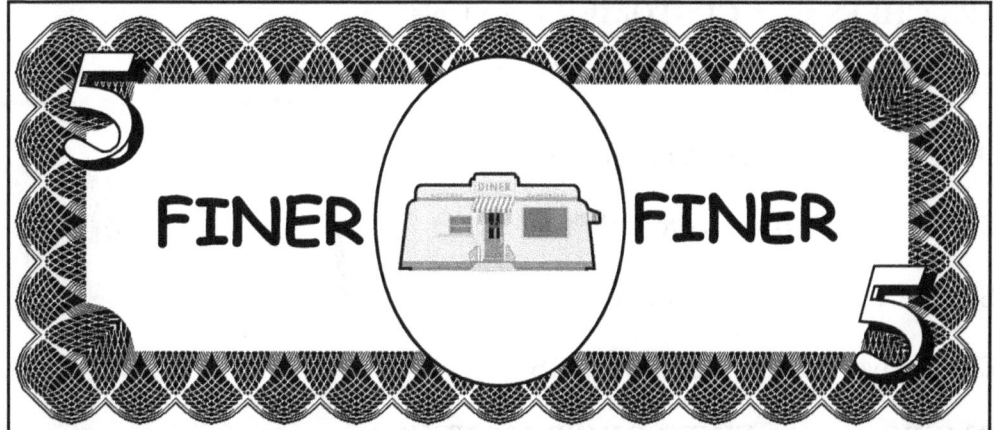

Language

IF I WERE YOU

Plays Roles

Activity 2
Play HOW WAS YOUR DAY?

Goal
Demonstrate recall of details of the role play

Children should spend some time **ROLE PLAYING** at the **FINER DINER** (using templates and cut-outs on previous pages). If children need help with role-playing, **ENCOURAGE** them to enact the following:

- **SERVERS/CHEFS** greet **CUSTOMERS**

- **SERVERS/CHEFS** show **CUSTOMERS** to a table

- **SERVERS** hand out menus

- **CUSTOMERS** place food orders with **SERVERS**

- **SERVERS** deliver food orders to **CHEFS**

- **CHEFS** prepare pretend food (use food props/plates)

- **SERVERS** deliver food to **CUSTOMERS**

- **CUSTOMERS** pay with **FINER DINER MONEY**

- **SERVERS/CHEFS** say goodbye to **CUSTOMERS**

TEACHER TIP
Consider a field trip to a real diner before doing this activity. Or make simple diner fare (like pancakes) in the classroom

Language

IF I WERE YOU
Plays Roles

After ROLE PLAYING at the FINER DINER . . .

    GATHER children around in a circle and give each an opportunity to tell **HOW WAS YOUR DAY**?

- What role did you play today? (chef, server, customer)
- What were your duties as chef . . . server. . . customer?
- Were you busy? Did you work hard? Did you enjoy your work?
- Did you have fun as a customer? What kind of food did you order?
- Did you find any of your favorite foods on the menu?

Budding Learners:

Encourage budding learners to be "customers" first time around. Then switch roles once they learn the different diner "duties."

Blossoming Learners:

Encourage servers to help their customers "read" the menus and offer suggestions. Help them fill out order forms and use money.

Language

KNOCK, KNOCK, TICK, TOCK
Discriminates Consonants

Activity 1
Learn about **SAME SOUNDS**

Goal
Learn to identify different consonants by listening for "same sounds"

LET'S READ!

READ *CHICKEN IN THE CHURCH CLOCK* on the next page. Then discuss . . .

- Let's get ready to play SPOT THE SAME SOUNDS. How many <s> sounds do you hear when I say "Spot The Same Sounds"?

- Do you hear same sounds when I say: "Knock, Knock, Tick, Tock, Cluck, Cluck"? What are they? (<n>, <t>, <k>)

- Do you hear the same sounds when I say: "Chicken in the Church Clock?" What are they?

- These same sounds we hear at the beginning and end of words are called consonants.

> **TEACHER TIP**
> When discussing consonants, this book will use <k> to represent "k" or "hard c" sound. For discussions with children about consonants, when you see the letter "k" written as <k>, say the sound rather than saying the letter ("kay"). And when you see <ch>, say the sound that "ch" makes rather than saying the letters ("c,h") and so on . . .

Language

KNOCK, KNOCK, TICK, TOCK
Discriminates Consonants

Knock, Knock
Tick, Tock,
Cluck, Cluck . . . Choo!
Chicken in the church clock
Sneezed at you

Knock, Knock,
Tick, Tock,
Cluck, Cluck . . . Who?
Chicken's dressed for Halloween,
A ghostly goblin . . . BOO!

Knock, Knock
Tick, Tock,
Tap, Tap, Tap . . .
Time to tell chicken to
Take a nap!

Language

KNOCK, KNOCK, TICK, TOCK

Discriminates Consonants

Activity 2
Play Spot THE SAME SOUNDS

Goal
Find and identify consonant sounds

Knock, Knock
Tick, Tock,
Cluck, Cluck . . .
Choo!
Chicken in the church
clock
Sneezed at you

SPOT THE SAME SOUNDS!

- How many <n> sounds do you hear?

- How many <t> sounds do you hear?

- How many <k> sounds do you hear?

- How many <ch> sounds do you hear?

Language

KNOCK, KNOCK, TICK, TOCK
Discriminates Consonants

Knock, Knock,
Tick, Tock,
Cluck, Cluck . . .
Who?
Chicken's dressed for Halloween,
A ghostly goblin . . . BOO!

SPOT THE SAME SOUNDS!

- How many \<n\> sounds do you hear?

- How many \<t\> sounds do you hear?

- How many \<k\> sounds do you hear?

- How many \<h\> sounds do you hear?

- How many \<g\> sounds do you hear?

Language

KNOCK, KNOCK, TICK, TOCK
Discriminates Consonants

Knock, Knock
Tick, Tock,
Tap, Tap,
Tap . . .
Time to tell chicken to
Take a nap!

SPOT THE SAME SOUNDS!

- How many <n> sounds do you hear?

- How many <t> sounds do you hear?

- How many <k> sounds do you hear?

- How many <h> sounds do you hear?

- How many <P> sounds do you hear?

MIND STRETCHERS

Budding Learners:

As budding learners identify consonant sounds, next ask them to "name the letter." Example: The <t> sound comes from letter "tee."

Blossoming Learners:

Ask blossoming learners to identify whether a same sound comes at the beginning or end of a word.

Language

KNOCK, KNOCK, TICK, TOCK

Discriminates Consonants

Activity 3
Chicken Chat

Goal
Create same sounds

Help the chicken finish the verse by making our own **SAME SOUNDS**:

Knock, Knock,
Tick, Tock,
Peck, Peck,
PECK . . .

_____
_____!

Knock, Knock,
Tick, Tock,
Boom, Boom
BOOM . . .

_____
_____!

Language

Knock, Knock, Tick, Tock
Discriminates Consonants

Activity 4
Make Chicken Chat name tags

Goal
Create same sounds for your own name

- **USE** the template on the opposite page to create **CHICKEN CHAT NAME TAGS** for each child.

- **HELP** the child think of a word that begins with the **SAME SOUND** as his/her name and write it on the chicken (e.g., Generous Jason, Active Ashley, Brilliant Brittany . . .) Don't forget to make a teacher tag too!

- Then **INVITE** kids to **COLOR** and **DISPLAY** their very own **CHICKEN CHAT NAME TAGS**!

Activity 4
Read *Hand, Hand, Fingers, Thumb* by Al Perkins

Goal
Get more practice spotting same sounds

LETS READ!

In *HAND, HAND, FINGERS, THUMB*, Al Perkins has packed in plenty of clever consonants, like "dum ditty dum ditty dum dum dum" to keep kids entertained and learning. So many **same sounds** to spot!

Language

KNOCK, KNOCK, TICK, TOCK
Discriminates Consonants

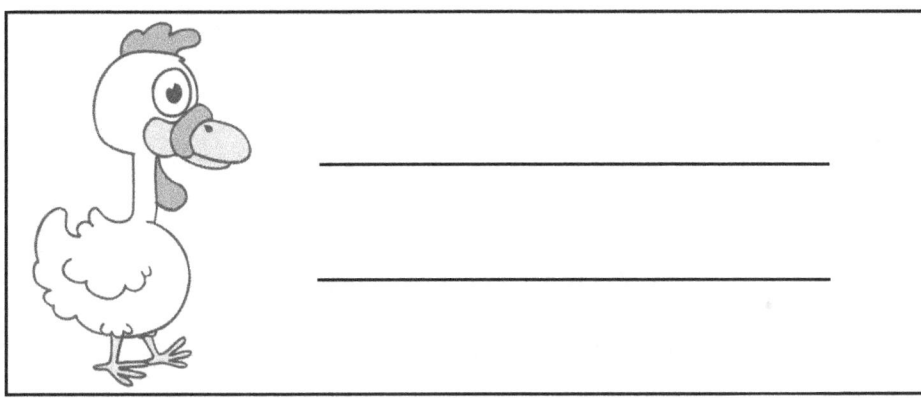

Examples

 **Lucky Lisa**

 **Gary the Great**

Language

YOU CAN SAY THAT AGAIN

Speaks Informally

Activity 1
Play ARE YOU TALKING TO ME?

Goal
Learn different greetings for different people

LET'S TALK!

- **EXPLAIN** to children that we use different greetings for different people we talk to.

- **ASK** children if they can guess why.

- Then **EXPLAIN** that most grown-ups (e.g., teachers, doctors, store clerks, etc.) like us to use our best-manners (or formal) voices. Friends and family like us to use our close-to-me (or informal) voices. But no matter who we talk to, we should always be **POLITE** and **KIND**.

LET'S PLAY!

- **CUT OUT** each of the characters depicted on the opposite page. (Templates are included at the end of this section). Paste characters to a board or lay them out on the floor or table (depending on how you'll be presenting to the children).

- **READ** each greeting and ask children to repeat it after you. Then point to each character (one at a time) and ask: **ARE YOU TALKING TO ME?**

(Note: There may be more than one right answer for each greeting.)

Language

YOU CAN SAY THAT AGAIN
Speaks Informally

Teacher Tina   Coach Carl   Doctor Dina   Uncle Max   Mom   Dad

Big Brother Brandon   Babysitter Sue   Baby Benny   Best Friend   School Buddies

Greetings/Sayings

- Hey, everyone!
- Thank you, Uncle Max!
- Got a sec?
- Yes, ma'am, I'm listening.
- What's for dinner?
- Wanna play?
- May I have some dessert?
- I'll see you next time, Doctor Dina.
- See ya later, alligator!
- Good morning, Miss Tina.
- I'm ready to play, Coach!
- Can I have a snack?
- Wave bye-bye.
- What's going on?
- Yes, sir. I understand.
- Can you come over?

- I'm hungry.
- Are there any more crayons?
- May I use the bathroom?
- Nice to meet you.
- Hi, guys!
- No-no, baby!
- Can you help me?
- Is it okay if I go outside?
- Hey, what's up?
- Good afternoon, sir.
- Can I have a snack?
- Careful. Don't get a boo boo.
- Want some?
- Will you please read a story?
- Can I stay up a little longer?
- I'm outta here!

Language

YOU CAN SAY THAT AGAIN
Speaks Informally

Activity 2
Play SAYS WHO?

Goal
Identify words/tones associated with different people

- **REINFORCE** idea that we can be more informal with our friends (using slang and "fun words") and with our family (sometimes using terms of endearment and special nicknames). But when we speak to other grown-ups, professionals, and strangers, it's best to start out using formal manners and words.

- Now that children have identified different ways to talk **TO** different people (Activity 1), let them try their hand at guessing who's talking in **Activity 2: SAYS WHO**?

- On the opposite page, **DRAW A LINE** from the character to the words s/he is most likely to be saying.

> **TEACHER TIP**
> Point out that nicknames or "sweet names" (terms of endearment) are used in the exercise. Ask kids if they have a special nickname or "sweet name" that their parents or family call them at home.

MIND STRETCHERS

Budding Learners:
Be sure to read words of dialogue aloud. Consider making this a group activity rather than handing out individual worksheets.

Blossoming Learners:
Ask if blossoming learners can identify slang words (e.g., wanna, gonna, dude, chow) and tell what they mean.

Language

YOU CAN SAY THAT AGAIN
Speaks Informally

Wanna sit with us?

Let's go to my house!

Dude! What's goin' on?

Chow time . . . Come and get it!

Are you getting sleepy, Honey?

Don't worry, young man. You're gonna be just fine.

Language

YOU CAN SAY THAT AGAIN
Speaks Informally

Language

YOU CAN SAY THAT AGAIN
Speaks Informally

105

Cognitive

Unit 3
Developmental Activities

'Tis The Season
Knows seasons

Pencil Portraits
Draws person

You're Out Of Order
Classifies objects

Are You For Real?
Recognizes fantasy

What If
Recognizes cause and effect

Who Knew
Predicts outcomes

What's In A Year
Identifies months

Look At The Time
Recognizes clock numbers

Cognitive

TIS THE SEASON
Knows Seasons

SWIRL-A-YEAR

Crispy leaves float
As the autumn air cools.
Children yell trick-or-treat,
Dressed up as ghouls.

Cool air turn colder.
As flakes float on breezes,
Mom makes hot chocolate
To soften our sneezes.

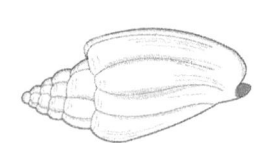

Flakes upon flakes
Make for mountains of white;
Praying for school closings
All through the night.

Snow turns to puddles.
Soft tulips reach high,
Stretching pink faces
Toward blue and white sky.

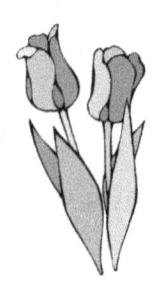

Wind blows the clouds away;
Sunlight peeks through.
Out come the bicycles;
Roller skates, too.

School days have ended.
Hot summer is here.
Lazy days dangling my
Feet off the pier.

Seagulls soar overhead;
Sand warms my toes.
Waves crashing harder now.
Chilly wind blows

Through sandcastle walls
By the cool salty reef.
Carrying with it
Fall's first crispy leaf.

Cognitive

TIS THE SEASON
Knows Seasons

Activity 1
Read and Discuss *SWIRL-A-YEAR*

Goal
Learn that the seasons of the year are cyclical

LET'S READ & TALK!

- **READ** *SWIRL-A-YEAR* aloud two times.

- **ASK** for answers to the following questions:

  - How does the poem begin? (What is floating in the breeze?)

  - How does the poem end? Why do you think the poem begins and ends with the leaf? (Introduce the idea that the seasons go round and round from one year to the next. The seasons pass but they always come back again.)

  - How many seasons are there? Can you name them all?

  - What happens in the Winter? Spring? Summer? Fall?

Cognitive

'Tis The Season

Knows Seasons

Activity 2
Season Match-Up

Goal
Know which clothing and activities belong to each season

SEASON MATCH-UP

Find the picture that does NOT belong with the season shown in box at the left. Can you name the season?

110

Cognitive

Tis The Season

Knows Seasons

Activity 2
Learn a Simple Season Rhyme

Goal
Memorize the seasons in order

SEASONS

Springtime showers bring us <u>flowers</u>.
Sun in summer helps them <u>grow</u>.
Fall turns leaves to red and <u>brown</u>.
And chilly winter brings us <u>snow</u>.

Teacher Tip
Try it with gestures!
On Springtime Showers . . . wiggle fingers like rain falling from sky.
On bring us flowers . . . palms together, then open like budding flower.
On sun in summer . . . arms in circle over head for sunshine.
On fall turns leaves . . . fingers open wide, palms facing outward, swaying like leaves on a breeze.

MIND STRETCHERS

Budding Learners:

Budding learners may prefer to listen to teacher recite the rhyme while they follow along with gestures only.

Blossoming Learners:

To help blossoming learners memorize the rhyme, try leaving out the underlined words (above) for them to fill in for you.

Cognitive

PENCIL PORTRAIT
Draws Person

Activity 1
Meet Nick the Stick Man

Goal
Know the main parts of the human figure
NOTE: Also practice motor skills by assembling
a simple five-piece puzzle

WE CAN REBUILD HIM!

- **GATHER** children in small groups (2-3).

- **GIVE** each group six pipe cleaners:
    - One is formed into a circle (head)
    - Four are straight and of equal size (arms, legs)
    - One is straight and slightly longer (body)

- **INVITE** children to put the pieces together to make Nick the Stickman.

- After each group has built their own Nick, **INVITE** them to get creative and bend arms, legs, body into different positions.

- **POINT OUT** and applaud instances where they've created elbows, knees, hands and feet.

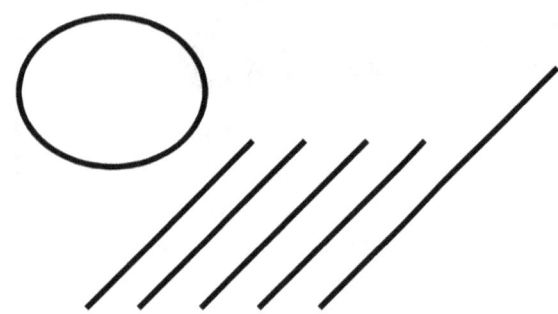
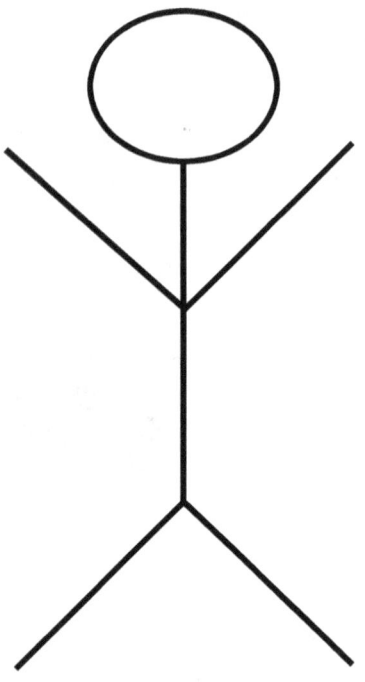

Cognitive

PENCIL PORTRAIT
Draws Person

Activity 2
Make a Pencil Portrait

Goal
Draw human figure with details

LET'S DRAW!

- **GIVE** each child a pencil and a sheet of blank paper.

- **ASK** them to draw Nick **VERY LIGHTLY** in pencil.

- **GIVE** each table some crayons or colored markers. **INSTRUCT** them to fill in Nick's features and clothing **ONE DETAIL AT A TIME**. Examples:
  - "Let's give Nick some eyes. What else goes on Nick's face?"
  - "Now let's put some clothes on Nick. He needs a shirt."
  - "Let's give Nick some pants." (Or if Nick is Nikki, perhaps a skirt. Kids can choose either gender.)
  - "Nick needs some shoes . . . hair. . . etc. . . . "

- Be sure to have the children draw right on top of the pencil outline with their markers. The pencil outline is only meant to serve as a guide. After they dress Nick and fill in the details, they'll be surprised at the result.

MIND STRETCHERS

Budding Learners:
It may be helpful for budding learners to see simple cartoon drawings of people to help inspire ideas as they add details to Nick.

Blossoming Learners:
Encourage blossoming learners to draw another person picture . . . this time WITHOUT the pencil portrait of Nick underneath.

Cognitive

You're Out Of Order

Classifies Objects

Activity 1
Upside-Down Classroom

Goal
Understand everyday order and groupings

Let's Discover!

- **BEFORE** kids arrive in the morning, make some obvious alterations to the classroom -- set things out of order. Examples can include the following, but get creative and do what works for your classroom:
    - Hang paper towels on coat rack pegs.
    - Put plastic spoons in the crayon boxes. Set crayon boxes out on tables where they'll be discovered.
    - Put books in cubbies.
    - Set toys on chairs.

- **ALLOW** kids to discover the disorder and, when they do, teacher should pretend to be as baffled as they are.

- **ASK WHY** each each example doesn't make sense:
    - Why don't the paper towels belong here?
    - Where do they belong?
    - How did you notice this spoon doesn't belong?
    - What is a spoon used for? What is a crayon used for?
    - Why don't the books belong in the cubbies? What <u>does</u> belong here?
    - Where do these toys belong? Why?

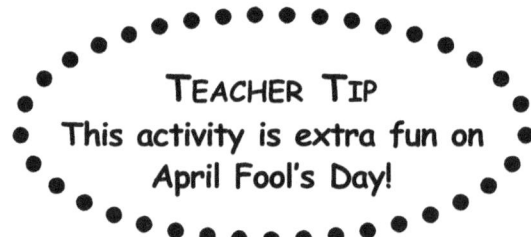

Teacher Tip
This activity is extra fun on April Fool's Day!

Cognitive

YOU'RE OUT OF ORDER
Classifies Objects

Activity 2
Noodle Caboodle

Goal
Sort items into sets, matching them according to shape and size

LET'S SORT!

- **FILL** a plastic freezer bag with 3-6 different types of pasta. Recommended shapes:

- **SHOW** the kids your **NOODLE CABOODLE** -- a collection of different types of noodles -- and ask for their help sorting the noodles into groups by shape/size in time for your big dinner party tonight.

- Provide **BOWLS** to hold their sorted noodles.

- Be sure to **PRAISE** them for a job well done. Your dinner is sure to be a hit!

   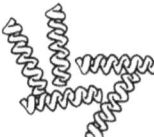  

MIND STRETCHERS

Budding Learners:
After sorting, ask blossoming learners to divide noodles into smaller groups of five to help improve their counting skills.

Blossoming Learners:
Try this activity with alphabet pasta or cereal shapes. Blossoming learners will have fun sorting them into piles.

Cognitive

ARE YOU FOR REAL?

Recognizes Fantasy

Activity 1
Read and discuss *THE BIONIC BUNNY SHOW* by Marc Brown

Goal
Differentiate between real and imaginary characters and settings

LET'S READ!

Marc Brown's *THE BIONIC BUNNY SHOW* gives kids a sneak peek behind the scenes of a TV show featuring a well-known super hero bunny!

LET'S TALK!

- Begin a discussion of *THE BIONIC BUNNY SHOW* by **ASKING** children about the main character (in both real and super hero form):
    - Who is Wilbur Rabbit? Who is The Bionic Bunny?
    - How does Wilbur become The Bionic Bunny?
    - Is The Bionic Bunny a real or made-up character?
    - What's the difference between a real person/bunny and a super hero?

- Next **ASK** kids to consider how TV and movies (and even storybooks) can make pretend characters seem real.
    - Who is your favorite pretend character (in books, on TV, in movies)?
    - Is that character real? How do you know?
    - Do you like to pretend you're that character?
    - How does that make you feel?

- **EXPLAIN** that when you "pretend" or play "make believe," that's the same thing an actor does when playing a character on TV or in a movie.

Cognitive

ARE YOU FOR REAL?
Recognizes Fantasy

Activity 2
Create a fantasy land and then a story

Goal
Learn the elements of a fantasy story

LET'S CREATE!

- **GATHER** children for a story circle. **INVITE** them to create a new story -- this time a **fantasy** -- using the same and-then technique learned in OUT OF MY HEAD section of this book.

- **ENCOURAGE** kids to include as many elements of fantasy as possible (e.g., superheroes, wizards, monsters, unicorns, fairies, magic wands, etc.)

- When the story ends, **INVITE** children to recall the make-believe parts of the story, and talk about what makes them make-believe instead of real.

- Ask them to **CONSIDER** whether a story can have both real and fantasy elements. Which parts of our story could be real? Which could not?

MIND STRETCHERS

Budding Learners:
Instead of inventing a fantasy story, budding learners may prefer picking out the fantasy elements in a familiar fairy tale.

Blossoming Learners:
Ask blossoming learners to name other fantasy stories they know and like (e.g., Cinderella, Three Little Pigs, Hansel & Gretel. . .)

Cognitive

> ## WHAT IF
> Recognizes Cause and Effect
>
> ### Activity 1
> Read and discuss FUN E. FRIENDS BOOK SERIES
> ### Goal
> Learn that by changing behaviors and qualities, we can change outcomes

LET'S READ!

Al Newman's **FUN E. FRIENDS** books are not only entertaining, but they also empower preschoolers to take an active role in instructing the Friends on how to overcome the fears and behaviors that need some changing.

FRAID E. CAT needs a friend to help her overcome her fear of the dark.

GRUB E. DOG sure could use some help with his terrible grooming habits.

FIBBER E. FROG would realize his friends will like him just the way he is, if only he could stop all that fibbing.

GIGGLE E. GOOSE has a great little giggle, but she needs to know when to let it out and when to keep it in check.

All these Fun E. Friends "need your help!"

As kids discover that a little of their very own advice can work wonders for these clever characters, they also learn a lesson in how to change outcomes by changing behaviors.

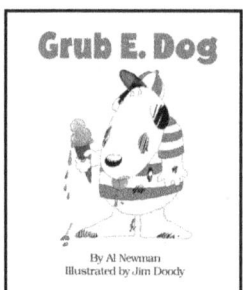
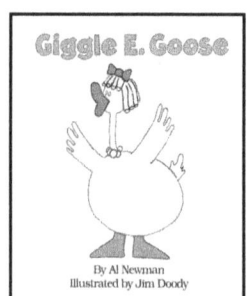

Available from www.humanicslearning.com

Cognitive

WHAT IF
Recognizes Cause and Effect

LET'S TALK!

WHAT IF FRAID E. CAT checked for monsters under her bed?

- What causes **FRAID E. CAT** to be afraid?
- Imagination can be great! But it can also make you scared.
- Are there really monsters under her bed?
- When **FRAID E. CAT** knows for sure the monsters are make-believe and not real, does she feel better?
- What did we do to help her stop being afraid?

CAUSE/EFFECT LESSON
Imagining scary make-believe things can cause you to be afraid.

Facing what's real (looking under your bed) can help you stop being afraid.

WHAT IF GRUB E. DOG had a tidy-up checklist?

- What causes **GRUB E. DOG**'s friends to hold their noses?
- Can **GRUB E. DOG** make changes to help his friends feel differently about him?
- Why is the tidy-up check list helpful to **GRUB E. DOG**?
- What changes does **GRUB E. DOG** make?
- What different things do you think will happen to **GRUB E. DOG** now that he's made these changes?

CAUSE/EFFECT LESSON
Being messy can cause people to not want to be around you.

Cleaning up your act can cause people to feel more comfortable spending time with you.

It can also help you feel better about yourself.

Cognitive

WHAT IF
Recognizes Cause and Effect

WHAT IF FIBBER E. FROG knew you liked him just the way he was?

- What kind of fibs does **FIBBER E. FROG** tell?
- Why does **FIBBER E. FROG** tell so many fibs?
- What if **FIBBER E. FROG** told his friends he was just a poor from who lived in a ditch? Would they still like him? Would you still like Fibber?
- What might happen if **FIBBER**'s friends found out he was fibbing?
- Is fibbing a good way to make friends?

CAUSE/EFFECT LESSON
Wishing you were more important might cause you to tell lies.
Telling lies might cause you to lose friends. People will stop trusting you.
Telling the truth will cause people to trust you!

WHAT IF GIGGLE E. GOOSE thought twice before speaking or giggling?

- When is giggling and chatting okay?
- Where are some places you should not giggle or chat out loud?
- What might happen if you giggle or chat in the wrong place?
- What will happen to **GIGGLE E. GOOSE** if she chatters in class? . . . at the movies?
- How do you think it makes someone feel if you chatter about them? . . . if you giggle about them?

CAUSE/EFFECT LESSON
Chattering or giggling in the wrong place can get you in trouble.
Giggling about someone can cause him/her to feel hurt.
Doing less chatting and giggling and more listening and paying attention can help you learn more.

Cognitive

WHAT IF
Recognizes Cause and Effect

Activity 2
Bold Mold

Goal
Understand cause and effect in the natural world

LET'S DISCOVER!

- **EXPLAIN** that cause and effect happen every day in the natural world.

- **SHOW** a simple cause-and-effect example by **growing mold**. Here's how:

    - Take two slices of plain sandwich bread.
    - Place one inside a zipped plastic sandwich bag and set in on a counter or table in the classroom.
    - Place the second inside a zipped plastic sandwich bag, along with 1 TBSP of water, and tape it to a sunny spot on a classroom window.
    - Watch the mold growth throughout the week. (Make this a daily task.)

- Kids will discover the moistened bread on the window grows mold more quickly (within a few days) than the non-moistened bread inside the classroom. This is because heat and water are two main causes of mold growth.

    heat + water = cause   mold = effect

MIND STRETCHERS

Budding Learners:
To give budding learners extra help with cause/effect concept, try demonstrating with a jack-in-the-box or bubble wrap.
(pushing=>popping!)

Blossoming Learners:
Ask blossoming learners to name some safety cause/effects: What can happen if you play with matches? . . . run on a slippery floor?

Cognitive

Who Knew

Predicts Outcomes

Activity 1
Blue Potato Experiment

Goal
Learn to make smart guesses

Let's Discover!

- **EXPLAIN** that a smart guess is a guess you make about what you think is going to happen based on things you already know.

- **ENCOURAGE** kids to "think like scientists," who often make smart guesses in their work. Today we're going to be scientists working in our classroom "lab" as we make smart guesses and discoveries about simple household items.

Smart Guess #1

What to do . . .	What to ask . . .
• Place two same-size see-through glass or plastic bowls on a desk or table in the "lab."	If we leave these two bowls on the table, what do you think will happen . . .
• Fill one bowl with ice	. . . to the bowl of ice? . . . to the bowl of water?
• Fill the other bowl with water, at least 5 cups	*Make a smart guess!*
NOTE: Begin this activity first thing in the morning.	NOTE: This activity requires some waiting and observation time

Cognitive

WHO KNEW
Predicts Outcomes

SMART GUESS #2

What to do . . .

- You should now have two clear bowls of water. (Be sure to talk about what happened to the ice/water. Were the smart guesses right?)

- Set 2 TBSP of aquarium pebbles next to water bowl #1

- Set 2 TBSP of salt next to water bowl #2

What to ask . . .

If we add these pebbles to this bowl of water, what do you think will happen?

If we add this salt to this bowl of water, what do you think will happen?

Make a smart guess!

Let the kids pour the pebbles into bowl #1, and the salt into bowl #2.

Were the smart guesses right?

SMART GUESS #3

What to do . . .

- Remove the pebbles from bowl #1. You now have two clear bowls of water again.

- Set 2 TBSP of red food coloring next to water bowl #1

- Set 2 TBSP of blue food coloring next to water bowl #2

What to ask . . .

If we add this red food coloring to this bowl of water, what do you think will happen?

If we add this blue food coloring to this bowl of water, what do you think will happen?

Make a smart guess!

Let the kids pour the red into bowl #1, and the blue into bowl #2.

Were the smart guesses right?

Cognitive

WHO KNEW
Predicts Outcomes

SMART GUESS #4

What to do . . .

- You should now have two clear bowls of colored water, one red, one blue.

- Set a dark colored (preferably polished) rock next to water bowl #1

- Set a peeled potato next to water bowl #2

What to ask . . .

If we add this rock to this bowl of water, what do you think will happen?

If we add this potato to this bowl of water, what do you think will happen?

Make a smart guess!

Let the kids set the rock into bowl #1, and the potato into bowl #2.

Were the smart guesses right?

After all of today's discoveries have been made, gather the "young scientists" for a re-cap of all the smart guesses. Ask them:

- How many of our smart guesses were correct?

- How were we able to make so many smart guesses?

- What new discoveries did we make today?

TEACHER TIP

Dress in a white lab coat on this day. And ask kids to bring in Mom or Dad's old white button-down shirt to wear as their own "lab coats." Lab goggles would be fun too (though not necessary).

Cognitive

WHO KNEW
Predicts Outcomes

TEACHER TIP

Wouldn't it be fun to serve blue potato chips as a special snack today? (You can find them at your local grocery store with the gourmet chips.) Ask the kids to guess where the blue potato chips come from.

Answer: They're made from naturally blue potatoes.

Cognitive

WHO KNEW
Predicts Outcomes

Activity 2
Plant a Potato

Goal
Make smart guesses about a long-term outcome.

MORE FUN WITH POTATOES

- **TRY** "planting" an unpeeled potato in a glass of water, held in place above the rim using toothpicks. (Stab the potato about halfway through its long side in four places.)

- **ASK** kids to make a smart guess about what will happen to the potato.

- Be sure to **OBSERVE** the potato at least 2-3 times per week so kids don't miss the first signs of growth (roots . . . and eventually leaves and stems)!

TEACHER TIP
This may be a child's first experience in a "lab" situation. It's great way to introduce them to the idea of problem statements and hypotheses (smart guesses) which will become important for school science fairs in a few years.

MIND STRETCHERS

Budding Learners:
Ask budding learners to think about what else can melt (ice cream cone, snowman. .) or dissolve in water (sugar, baby powder.)

Blossoming Learners:
Ask blossoming learners to predict what color you'll get if you mix the red water and the blue water. What about other color combinations?

Cognitive

WHAT'S IN A YEAR

Identifies Months

Activity 1
Learn a simple MONTHS OF THE YEAR song

Goal
Memorize the months of the year

SONG OF THE YEAR

(Sung to the tune of *OH MY DARLING CLEMENTINE*)

JANUARY, FEBRUARY,
MARCH and APRIL, MAY and JUNE.
They're the first months of the year and
So they start this little tune.

There's JULY and then there's AUGUST,
Then SEPTEMBER round the bend.
There's OCTOBER then NOVEMBER
And DECEMBER. That's the end.

TEACHER TIP
Have the kids count out the months on their fingers as they sing. Start with January on your first thumb, then hold up one finger every time the name of a month is sung. You'll have to re-use two fingers for the last two months, but kids will quickly catch on. They'll get used to the idea that there are 12 months in a year . . . and they'll eventually understand that 10 + 2 = 12.

Cognitive

What's In A Year

Identifies Months

Activity 2
Make a Month Wheel

Goal
Identify calendar months according to seasons

Let's Make A Wheel!

- **CUT** a large circle (at least 3' - 5' in diameter) from a sheet of mural paper.

- **DIVIDE** it into fourths (as shown below) using a thick felt marker. Then **LABEL** each section with the months of the year.

- **DRAW** winter, spring, summer and fall clouds to depict each month.

- **GIVE** crayons and markers to the kids and invite them to get down on the floor to decorate the month wheel with drawings of seasonal activities, drawing each in the corresponding section of the wheel.

- **USE** this creativity time to talk about which months fall in which seasons.

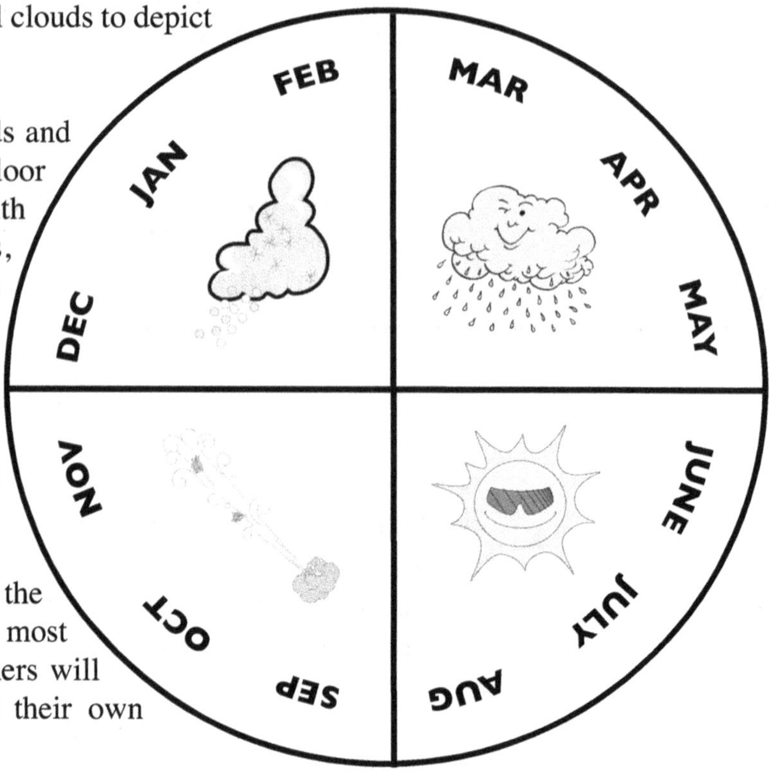

NOTE: The wheel pictured represents the typical seasonal break-down for most areas of the United States. Teachers will want to tailor the wheel to suit their own geographic variations.

Cognitive

LOOK AT THE TIME
Recognizes Clock Numbers

Activity 1
Clapping Time

Goal
Learn how many numbers are on a clock

RECITE AND LEARN!

ENCOURAGE kids to look at the classroom clock, or one you bring in to show (should be an analogue clock). **CLAP** out the numbers as you recite the following verse.

CLAPPING TIME
1, 2, 3, 4...
There's a clock above the door.
5, 6, 7, 8...
Are we early? Are we late?
9, 10, 11, 12
I can tell the time myself!

MIND STRETCHERS

Budding Learners:
Use a toy clock with moveable hands to show budding learners the positions for one o'clock, two o'clock, three o'clock..

Blossoming Learners:
Teach blossoming learners that big hand on twelve = the hour and big hand on six = the hour plus one-half (12:00 and 12:30).

Cognitive

LOOK AT THE TIME

Recognizes Clock Numbers

Activity 2
Clock Match-Up

Goal
Recognize the numbers on a clock

CLOCK MATCH-UP

Draw a line from the digital clock that matches the time on the analogue clock.

Motor Skills

UNIT 4
Developmental Activities

Piece It Together
Works puzzle

Cut It Out
Uses scissors

Copying Capitals
Copies uppercase letters

Skip Around
Skips

Heads Up
Catches ball

Put It In Reverse
Walks backwards

Write On!
Copies all letters

Family Portrait
Draws people

Motor Skills

PIECE IT TOGETHER
Works Puzzle

Activity 1
Shape It Up

Goal
Pieces together five simple shapes to form familiar objects

- Use the shape templates on the next page to cut shapes from different colored felt.
- Have children arrange the shapes on a flannel board to create different objects.

Here are some examples of what you can make!

Motor Skills

Piece It Together
Works Puzzle

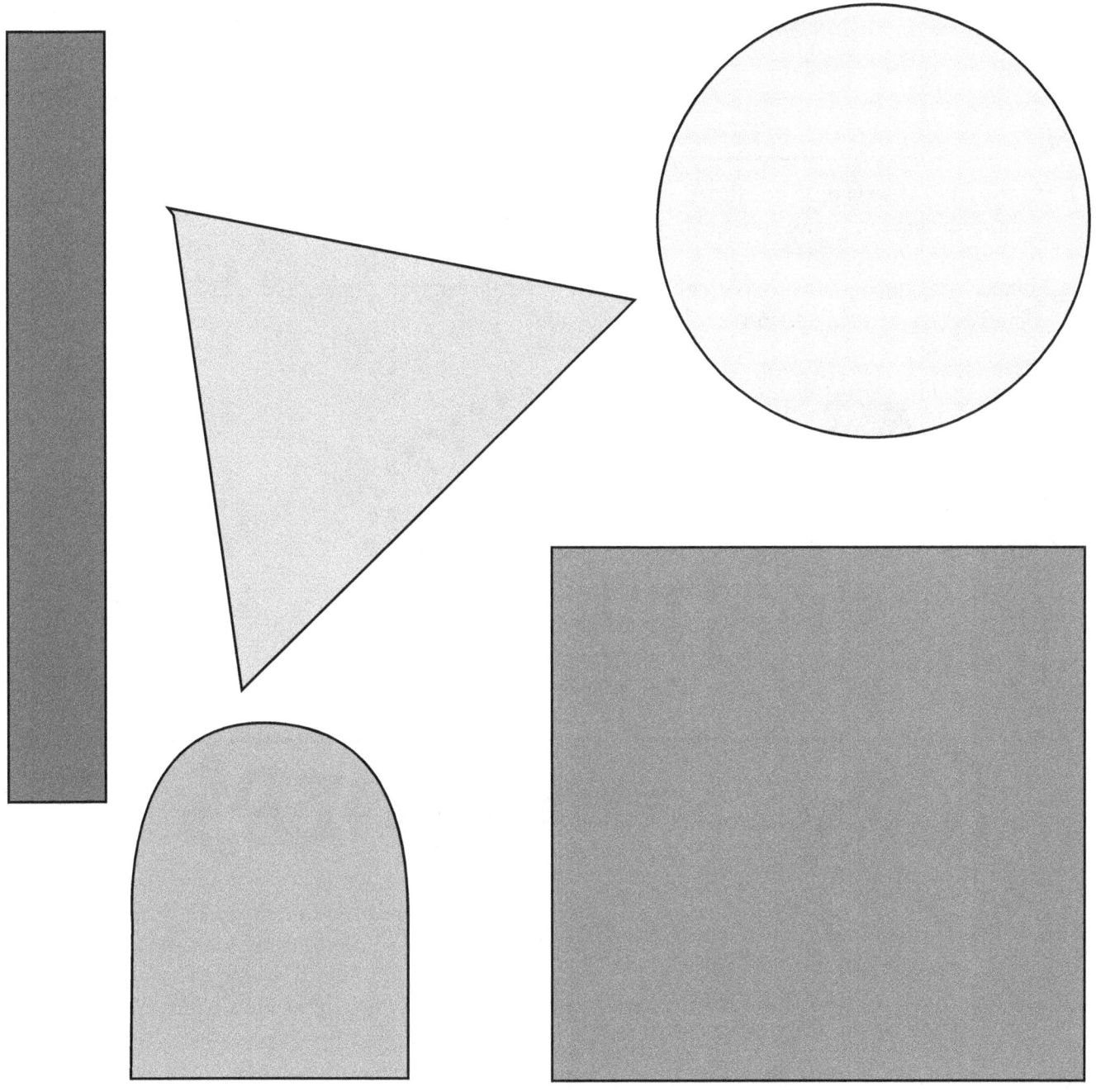

Motor Skills

PIECE IT TOGETHER
Works Puzzle

Activity 2
Create With Shapes

Goal
Turn simple shapes into art

- Next copy the shapes onto construction paper. Pass out scissors, glue sticks, colored markers, and one sheet of blank construction paper.

- Children can cut out the shapes, glue them onto construction paper, and add details with markers to create an even more artistic scene!

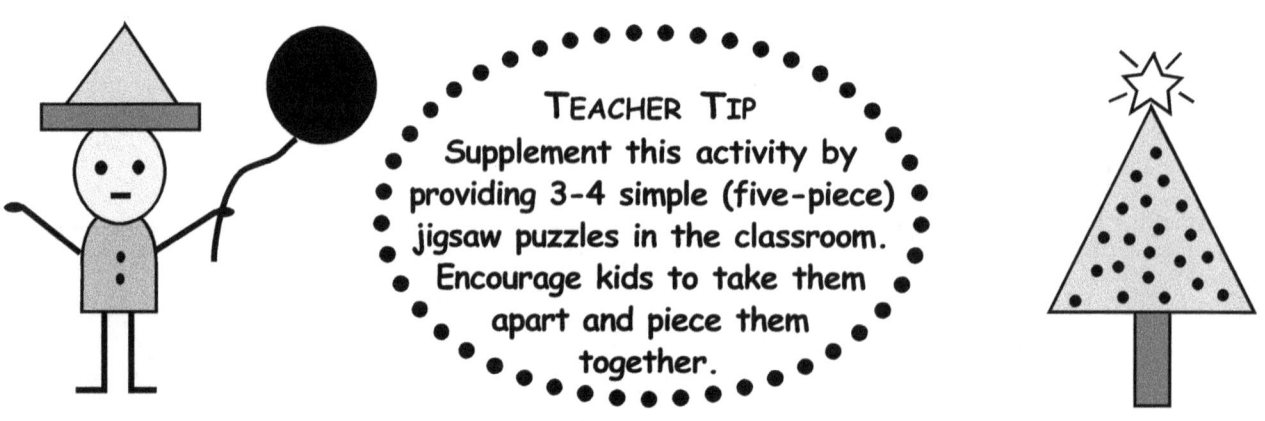

TEACHER TIP
Supplement this activity by providing 3-4 simple (five-piece) jigsaw puzzles in the classroom. Encourage kids to take them apart and piece them together.

MIND STRETCHERS

Budding Learners:
Prompt budding learners to create pictures with paper shapes by leaving the felt designs on display for them to see.

Blossoming Learners:
Give blossoming learners more than five shapes to try. Also provide shapes in varying sizes and see what they can create.

Motor Skills

CUT IT OUT
Works Puzzle

Activity 1
Piece Of The Pie

Goal
Cut in circles and along straight lines

MAKING PIZZA!

- **USE** the templates on the next page to make a pizza pie with toppings.

- **GIVE** children scissors, a glue stick and crayons or colored pencils/markers.

- Children will **MAKE THEIR OWN PIZZA PIES** (add fun toppings by using the template shapes or by drawing them on).

- Then they can **CUT** the pizza into slices to trade and share with friends.

MIND STRETCHERS

Budding Learners:
Budding learners might have more success drawing the toppings on the pie rather than cutting the smaller template pieces.

Blossoming Learners:
Ask blossoming learners how many slices equal half a pizza pie? How many equal one-fourth of a pizza pie?

Motor Skills

CUT IT OUT
Works Puzzle

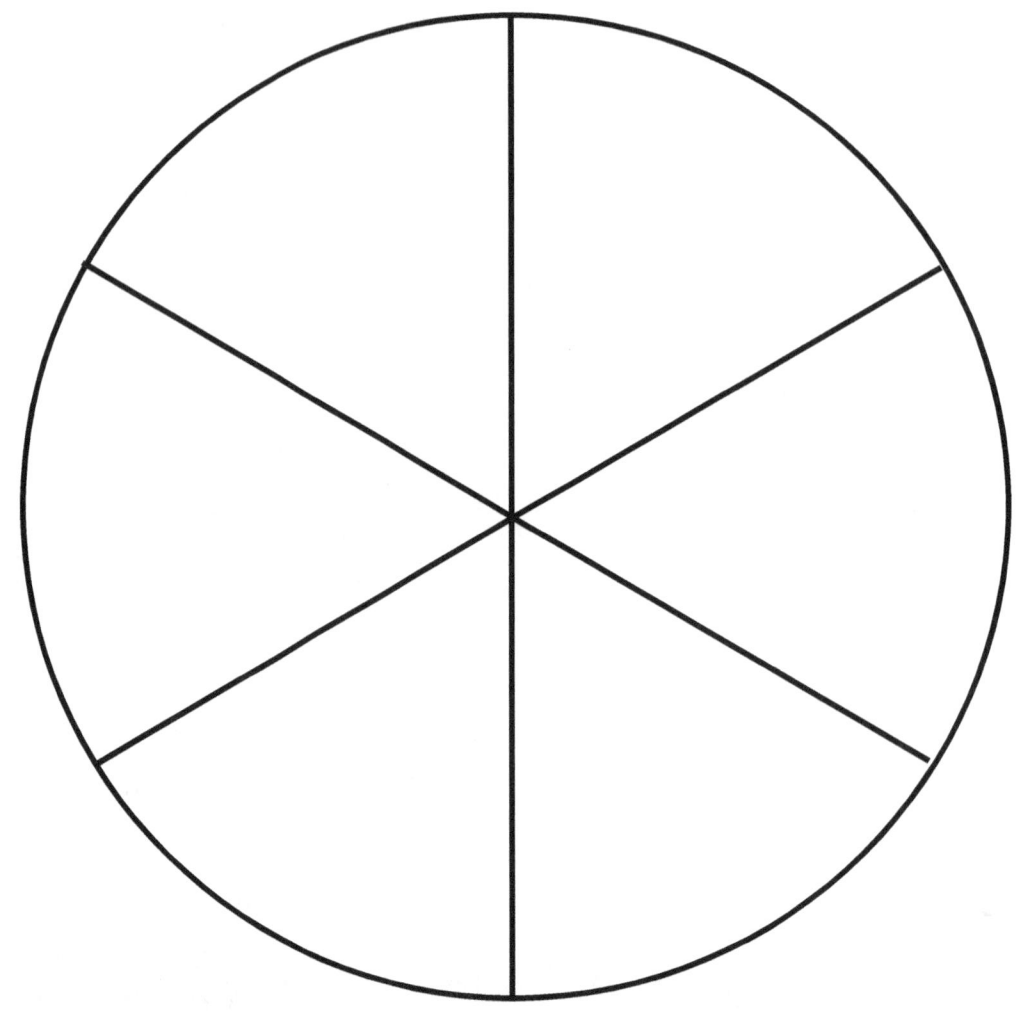

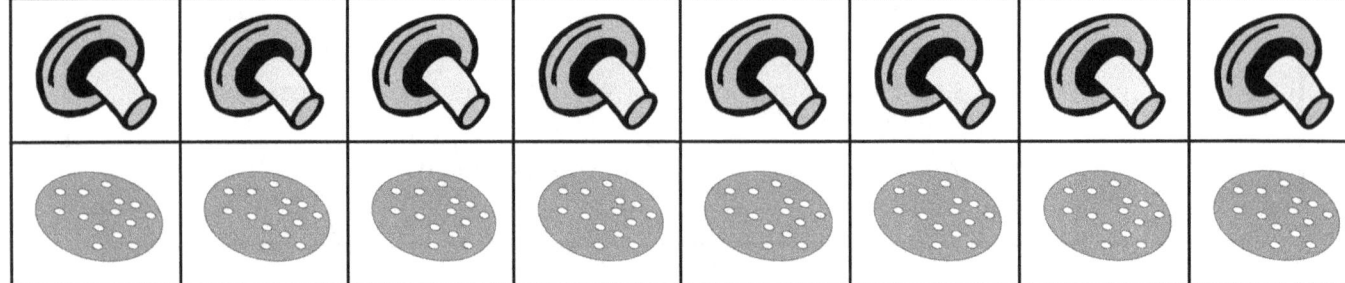

Motor Skills

CUT IT OUT

Works Puzzle

Activity 2
Scissor Sorcery

Goal
Get more practice with different kinds of cutting motions

Find more scissor activities, including over 100 reproducible templates and scissor safety rules in Sharon Bryant Carpenter's *SCISSOR SORCERY*.

SCISSOR SORCERY makes it easy to teach young scissor-users the six basic cutting motions:

- the snip
- the chop
- the sawmill
- the u-turn
- the poke
- the clip

Available from
www.humanicslearning.com

Motor Skills

COPYING CAPITALS
Copies Uppercase Letters

Activity 1
ABC Shapes

Goal
Learns to write letters by following lines and curves

LET'S WRITE!

- **GIVE** copies of the following **ABC PAGES** to each child -- one page per writing session, with the exception of the first one --- letter I, which can be combined with the next set of two-lined letters. It's best to do no more than one session per day.

- **READ** the rhyme for each letter set aloud two times.

- Children will then **TRACE** the letters.

- Let them **WRITE** as many as they can fit along the lines.

TEACHER TIP
Some children may need assistance with writing. It's best to move from table to table as they work to find out who needs help. Budding learners may only write one of each letter per session. Blossoming learners are likely to write three or more.

MIND STRETCHERS

Budding Learners:
Have budding learners trace over solid letters several times before trying to write the letter free-hand.

Blossoming Learners:
Encourage blossoming learners to write the letters free-hand on blank "railroad track" paper, without tracing.

Motor Skills

COPYING CAPITALS
Copies Uppercase Letters

This letter has 1 line.
It's straight up and down
Like a tower that stands
In the middle of town.

Motor Skills

COPYING CAPITALS
Copies Uppercase Letters

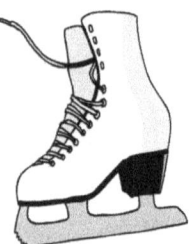
All these letters are made
Of 2 lines that are straight
Like the blade on the bottom
Of each winter skate.
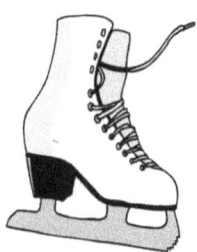

L

T

V

X

Motor Skills

COPYING CAPITALS
Copies Uppercase Letters

All these letters have **3** lines.
Just try and you'll see
how much fun drawing letters
with **3** lines can be!

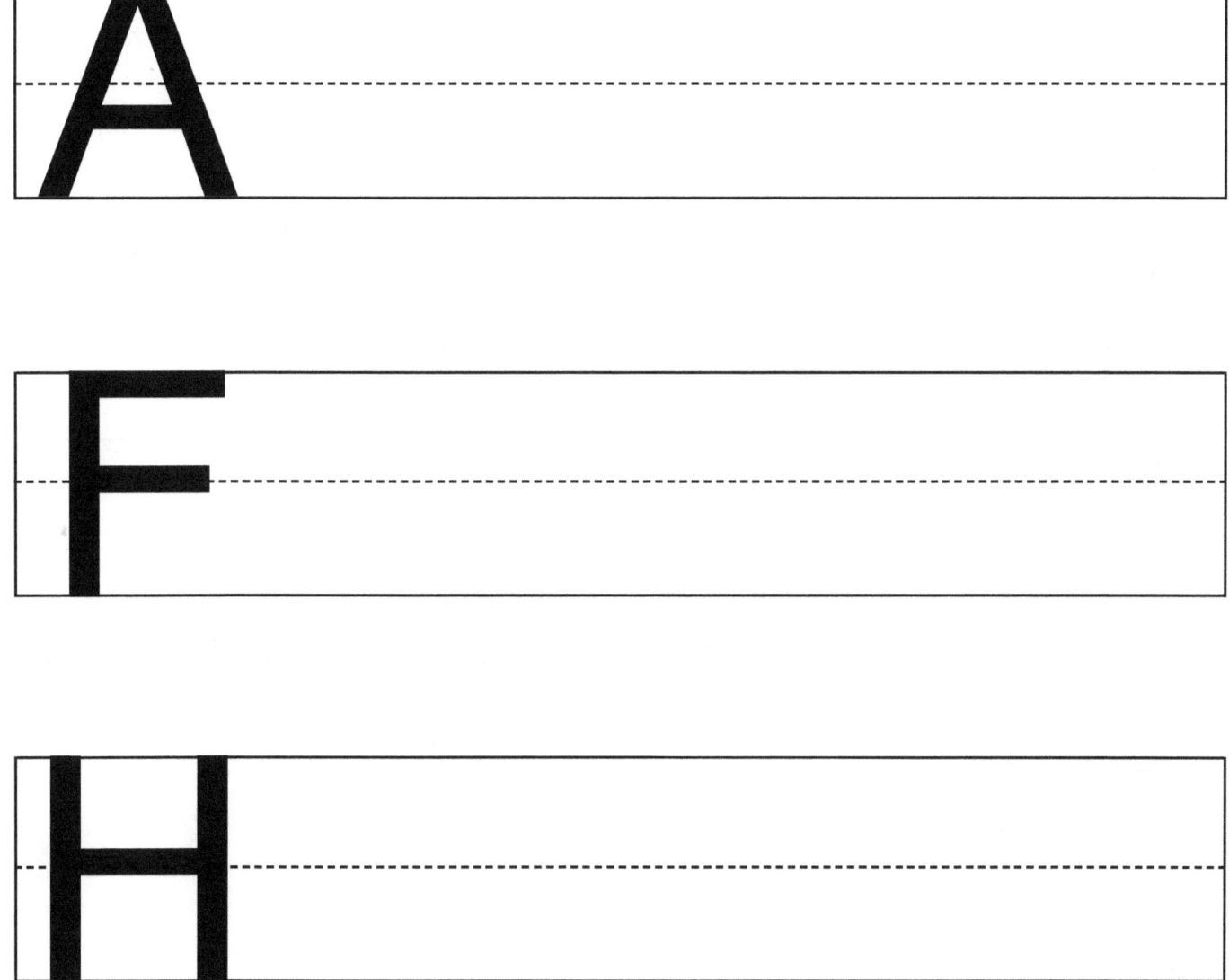

Motor Skills

COPYING CAPITALS
Copies Uppercase Letters

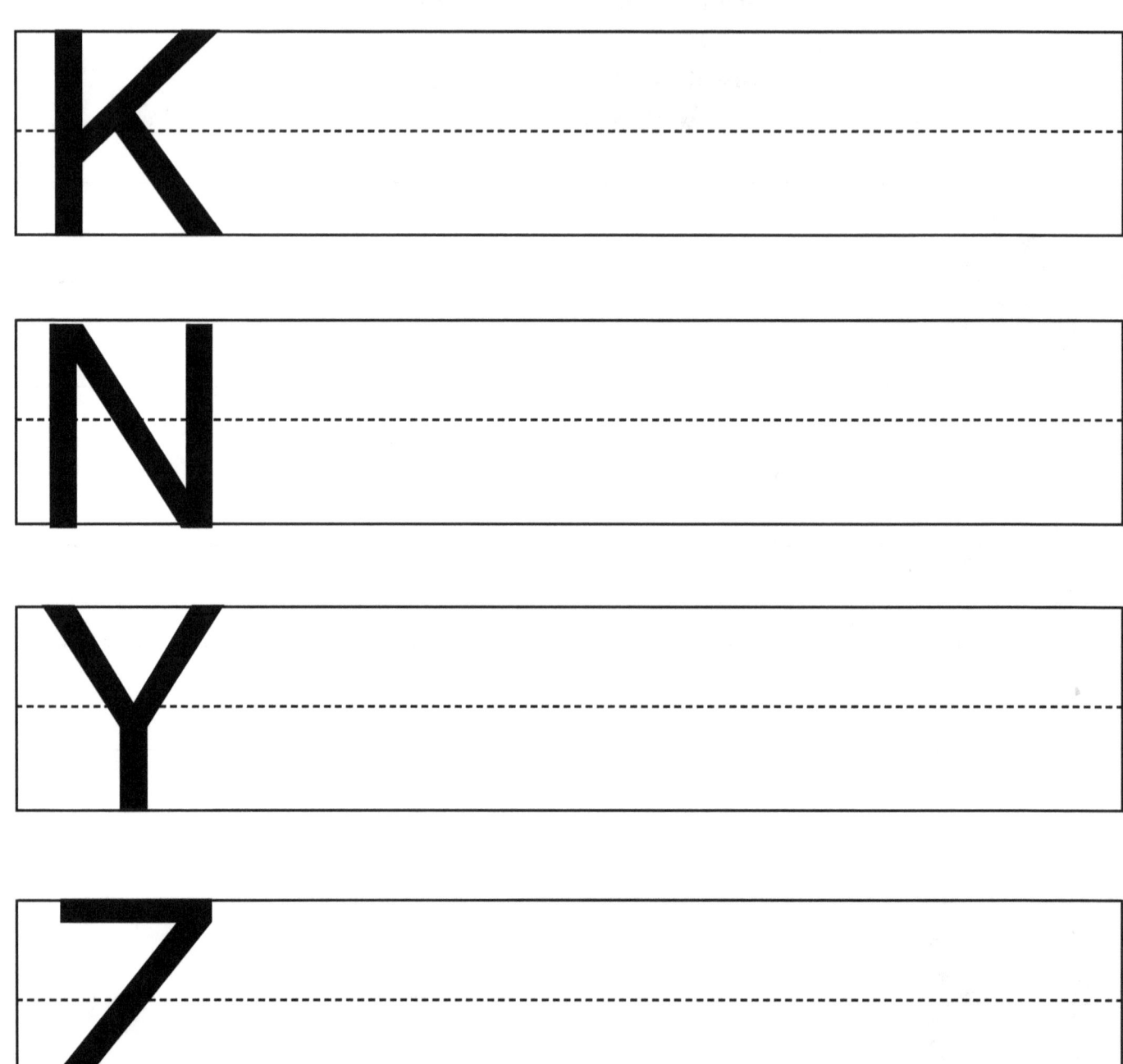

Motor Skills

COPYING CAPITALS
Copies Uppercase Letters

All these letters have **4** straight lines.
1 - 2 - 3 - 4
You won't find any letters
that have any more!

E

M

W

Motor Skills

COPYING CAPITALS
Copies Uppercase Letters

All these letters are curvy or round like a ball.
Watch your pencil point turn as you copy them all

C

J

O

S

U

Motor Skills

COPYING CAPITALS
Copies Uppercase Letters

All these letters are lucky,
And here's why that's true:
they have parts that are curvy
And straighter lines, too!

Motor Skills

COPYING CAPITALS
Copies Uppercase Letters

Motor Skills

> ### GET A MOVE ON
> **Skips**
>
> **Activity 1**
> **Skip & Rhyme**
>
> **Goal**
> Learn the skipping rhyme and skipping movements

RECITE AND LEARN!

- **READ** *SKIPPING TIME* aloud two times before adding any movements.

- Next, **DEMONSTRATE** skipping movements, using a bendable doll or your own body.

- **INVITE** kids to join in with their own skipping movements.

SKIPPING TIME

Right foot hop . . .
Left knee in air . . .
Left foot down
And hop right there!
Right knee up,
Then right foot down.
Now we're skipping
All around.

Motor Skills

GET A MOVE ON
Skips

Activity 2
Play A Skipping Version Of RED ROVER

Goal
Master skipping movements

LET'S PLAY!

Based on the classic game, RED ROVER, but using skipping instead of running, players do not "break through" an opposing line of children, making it a gentler game more suitable for five-year-olds.

Before beginning, lay out a "garden of clover" in front of each team's line. Use a non-slip welcome mat with a clover design or other non-slip green material to represent a clover garden.

- Children form two lines by holding hands. The lines face each other.

- One side starts by picking a person on the opposing team to skip over, and chants:

    Red Rover, Red Rover, send <Carlos> right over.
    Can <Carlos> skip over our garden of clover?

- As <Carlos> skips over, the other team counts his skipping steps:

    Skip one! Skip two! Skip three! Skip four . . . !

- If <Carlos> can skip all the way over, he chooses a player from the other team to add to his team. If he doesn't skip all the way, he joins the opposing team.

- Each team alternates until one team has all the players and is declared the winner. (This way everyone's a winner!)

Motor Skills

GET A MOVE ON
Skips

MIND STRETCHERS

Budding Learners:
Teach budding learners to gallop if they can't manage skipping movements. Then help them turn the gallop into a skip

Blossoming Learners:
While playing Red Rover, encourage blossoming learners to count their skips out loud as they skip along.

Motor Skills

HEADS UP!

Catches Ball

Activity 1
Read *THERE'S NO PLACE LIKE SPACE* by Tish Rabe

Goal
Learn that planets are varying distances from the sun (in preparation for PLANET BALL)

LET'S READ!

Before beginning Activity 2, **PLANET BALL**, read Tish Rabe's *THERE'S NO PLACE LIKE SPACE*, featuring Dr. Seuss's *CAT IN THE HAT* and friends (and written in Seuss rhyme). It's a quick introduction to the planets in our solar system. Understanding the different planets will enhance a child's experience playing **PLANET BALL**!

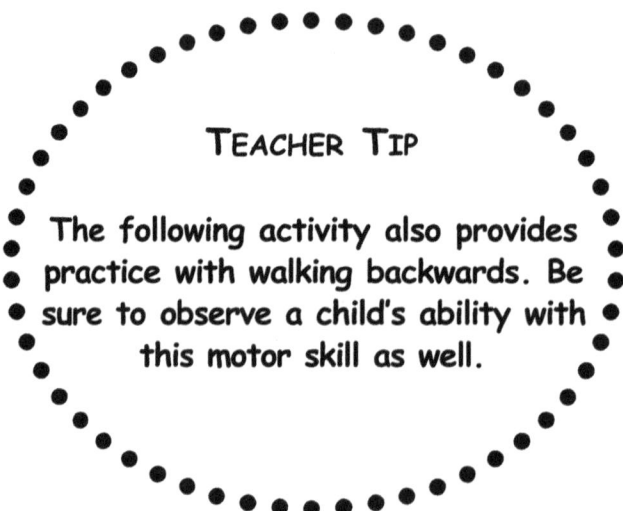

TEACHER TIP

The following activity also provides practice with walking backwards. Be sure to observe a child's ability with this motor skill as well.

Motor Skills

HEADS UP!
Catches Ball

Activity 2
Play PLANET BALL

Goal
Practice catching at changing distances

LET'S PLAY!

- Children form a circle standing around the teacher who is the **"sun"** in the center of all the children who are the **"Planets."**

- Each **planet** stands 3-4 feet from the **sun**. The **sun** tosses a whiffle-sized ball to the first **planet**, then the next, and so on, moving clockwise around the circle.

- As each **planet** successfully catches the ball, instruct him/her to toss it back and then take one big step backward away from the **sun**. If the **planet** misses the ball, he/she stays where he/she is and tries to catch again next time around.

- After several plays, the **planets** will have formed their own solar system as they stand at varying distances from the **sun**. Use this as an opportunity to point out who is close to the sun, like **Mercury**, **Venus**, and **Earth** . . . who is far away like **Pluto**, **Neptune** and **Uranus** . . . and who is in the middle like **Mars**, **Jupiter** and **Saturn**. This keeps the focus of the varying distances as a comparison to the different **planets**, and off the idea that some children are better catchers. And it allows the teacher to observe varying catching skills among children.)

MIND STRETCHERS

Budding Learners:
Use a larger ball (volleyball-size) for budding learners who have difficulty catching something smaller.

Blossoming Learners:
Encourage blossoming learners to take a turn playing the sun to get more practice catching and tossing.

Motor Skills

PUT IT IN REVERSE
Walks Backwards

Activity 1
Play A Game Of Stepping Stones

Goal
Practice walking backwards

PREPARATION

- Prepare several oval-shaped cut-out cards (about the size of index cards) in two or three different colored stacks. These are your colored "stepping stones."

- On each of the cards, write an instruction taken from the list below. You can have many duplicates of the same instruction.

SAMPLE INSTRUCTIONS

- Take 1 **baby** step forward
- Take 1 **giant** step forward
- Take 1 **baby** step backward
- Take 1 **giant** step backward
- Take 2 **baby** steps forward
- Take 2 **giant** steps forward
- Take 2 **baby** steps backward
- Take 2 **giant** steps backward
- Take 3 **baby** steps forward
- Take 3 **giant** steps forward
- Take 3 **baby** steps backward
- Take 3 **giant** steps backward

Motor Skills

Put It In Reverse
Walks Backwards

Let's Play!

- Line up all players at the far end of an indoor gym or playground, leaving at least six feet of space behind them. Stand at least 5-6 yards in front, facing them, with the colored stacks of cards ("**STEPPING STONES**") nearby.

- Working from left to right, ask each player in turn to choose a **STEPPING STONE** color. then read the instructions on the top card from that stack (i.e., if a player chooses "blue," pick a card from the blue stack and read the instruction.)

- The player steps forward or backward according to the **STEPPING STONE** instruction. The play then moves to the next player in line.

- Continue one player at a time, allowing each to choose a color, then reading the corresponding **STEPPING STONE** instruction.

- The first player to reach the goal line (that you have pre-set on the floor) or to get close enough to reach out and touch you, is the **WINNER**.

Mind Stretchers

Budding Learners:
Budding learners fearful of walking backward should step one foot back, then meet it with the other foot and pause before taking next step.

Blossoming Learners:
Include a stepping stone "challenge" pile (different color) with trickier instructions: *skip forward two steps, take one hop backward . . .*

Motor Skills

WRITE ON
Copies All Letters

Activity 1
Cut And Sort Letters

Goal
Review ABC letter shapes; practice cutting with scissors, sorting into groups, and working as a team

LET'S PLAY!

- Make groups of 2-4 children. Copy the letter templates on the next two pages and give a set to each group along with scissors for each child.

- Children cut out each letter box.

- Once all have been cut, children will work as a group to sort letters into piles based on letter shapes.

    - letters with straight lines only

    - letters with curves only

    - letters with both lines and curves

- Next, children will sort letters into piles of uppercase and lowercase. (NOTE: This version can be done on a separate day.

Motor Skills

WRITE ON
Copies All Letters

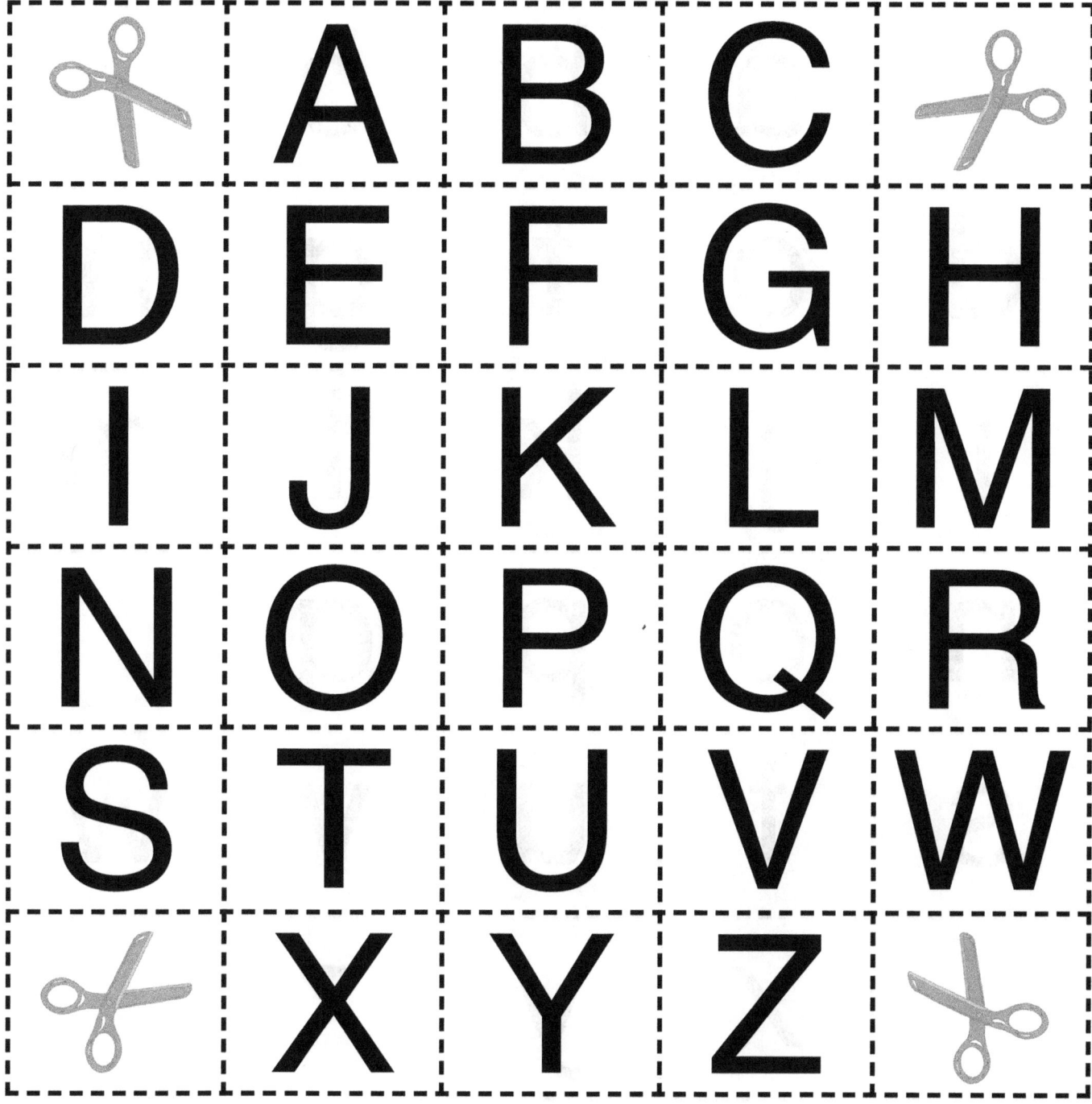

Motor Skills

WRITE ON
Copies All Letters

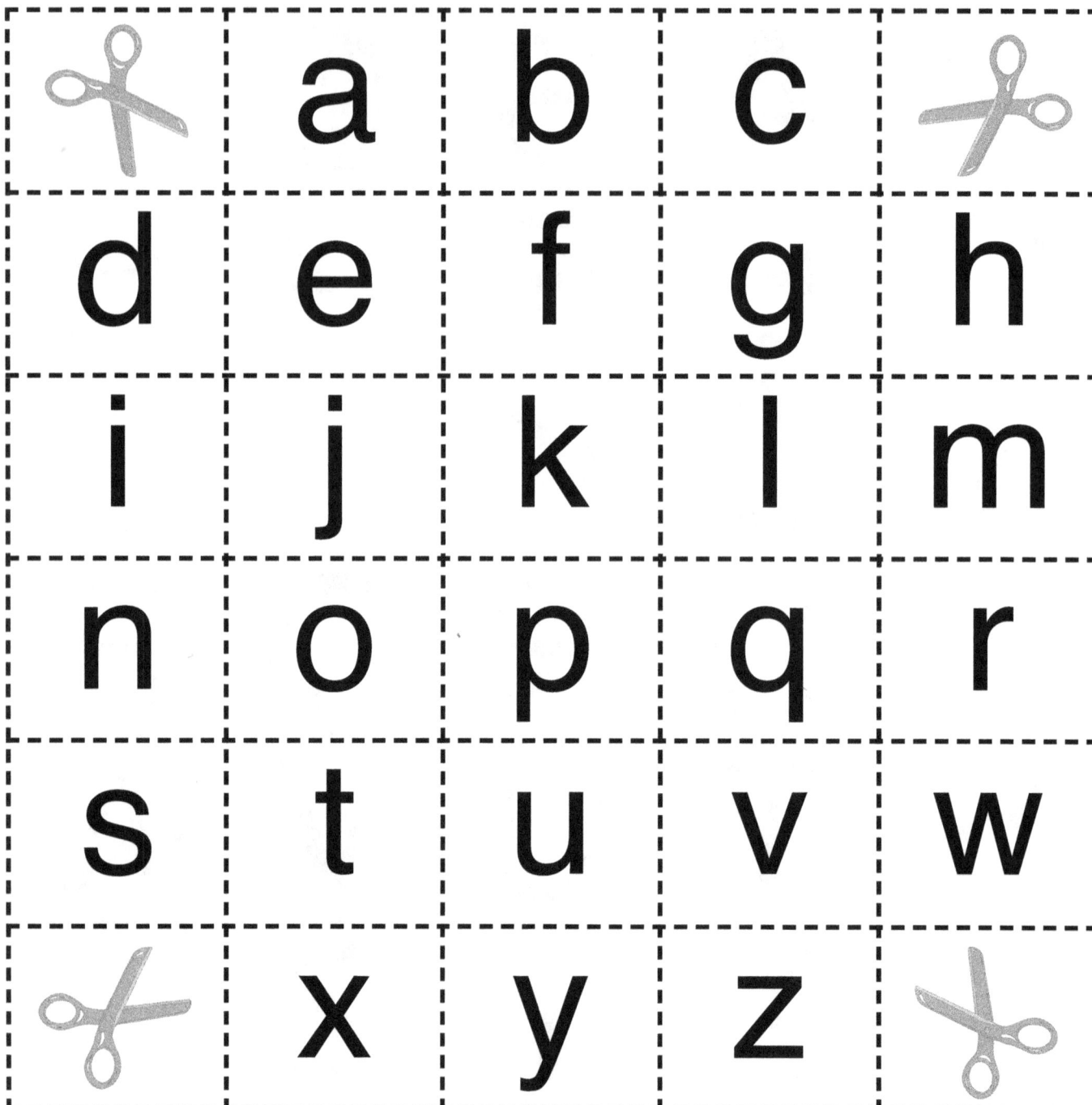

Motor Skills

WRITE ON
Copies All Letters

Activity 2
Letter Writing

Goal
Practice writing all letters of the alphabet

LET'S WRITE!

- Distribute lined paper and fat pencils.

- Children will copy letters onto the paper, using the cut-outs as a guide.

- Remind children to notice the different sizes and shapes of uppercase and lowercase letters.

TEACHER TIP
Refer back to Copying Capitals section to review different shapes for each letter. Re-read the rhymes describing letters with straight lines only, letters with curves and circles, and lucky letters that have both!

MIND STRETCHERS

Budding Learners:
Guide budding learners through sorting. Limit sorting to two piles: letters with straight lines only and letters with lines + curves.

Blossoming Learners:
Blossoming learners can sort letters into three piles: letter with straight lines only, letters with curves only, and letters with both.

Motor Skills

FAMILY PORTRAIT
Draws People

Activity 1
Fill In The Family

Goal
Practice drawing the human figure closer to scale

LET'S DRAW!

- **GATHER** children into circle time and talk about family.

    - How many are in your family?

    - Who is in your family?

    - What does your family like to do at home?

    - What does your family like to do when you go outside/to the park?

- **USE** the reproducibles on the following pages. Children can use crayons or colored pencils/markers to **DRAW THEIR FAMILIES IN THE PICTURES**. They can add their families to the home scene or the park scene, then have fun coloring in the rest of the picture.

Motor Skills

FAMILY PORTRAIT
Draws People

- Make special note of how much detail a child uses.

- Also note whether each figure is drawn to scale as a human form, and in comparison to the other objects in the picture (house, trees, park bench, etc.).

MIND STRETCHERS

Budding Learners:
Invite budding learners to draw themselves plus one other special family member if a "whole family" scene seems too overwhelming.

Blossoming Learners:
Look for a higher level of detail from blossoming learners. Encourage them to include a family pet, a favorite toy or the family car.

Motor Skills

FAMILY PORTRAIT
Draws People

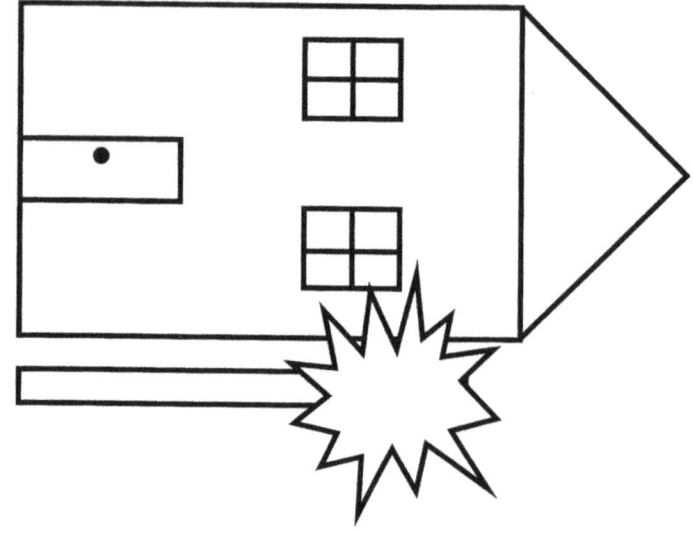

Motor Skills

FAMILY PORTRAIT
Draws People

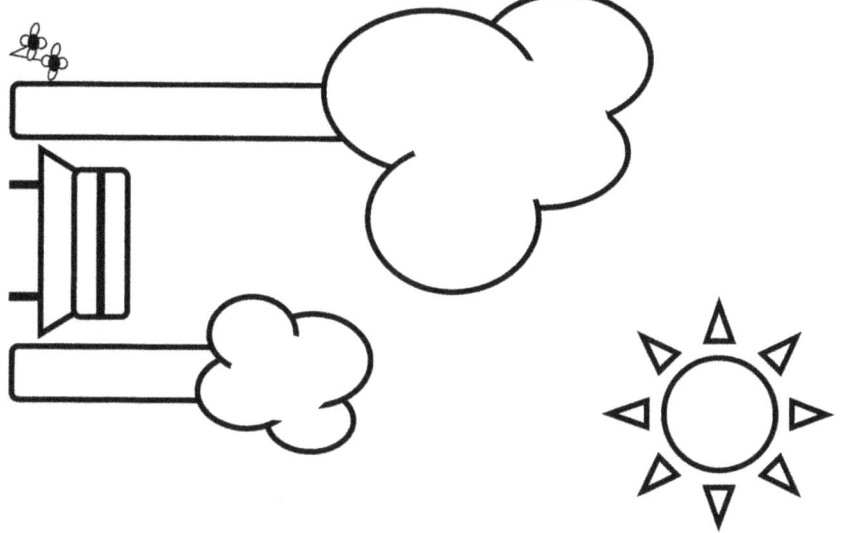

Motor Skills

Hygiene/Self-Help

UNIT 5
Developmental Activities

Take a Taste
Tries new food

What's To Eat
Identifies food

Play It Safe
Shows safety judgment

How's The Weather
Recognizes weather

Coming And Going
Understands travel

No Place Like Home
Knows address/phone number

Ready To Wear
Dresses self

Table Tools
Uses spoon and fork

Hygiene/Self-Help

TAKE A TASTE
Tries New Food

**Activity 1
Flavor Buffet**

Goal
Try familiar foods in different flavors

LET'S EAT!

- **SET** a buffet table with napkins, cups, paper plates and serving spoons.

- **CREATE** four food stations marked with table cards indicating each menu item:

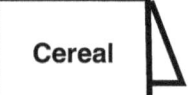  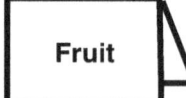 

- **SET OUT** three serving platters (reinforced paper plates are fine) for each food category, and three stacks of small paper cups for the juice category.

- **FILL** the buffet with the three choices in each category:

    - **Cereal**: corn, rice, wheat

    - **Crackers**: plain, whole wheat, pumpernickel

    - **Fruit**: watermelon, honeydew, cantaloupe (cut in squares)

    - **Juice**: apple, cranberry, grape (leave juice in bottles on display)

- **INVITE** kids to the **FLAVOR BUFFET**! Have them fill their paper plates with one of each item on the table (nine in all). Once they're seated, serve them three cups each of the different juices (filled only half way).

Hygiene/Self-Help

TAKE A TASTE
Tries New Food

Activity 2
Savor The Flavor

Goal
Describe different food flavors

LET'S TALK ABOUT TASTE!

- **ENCOURAGE** kids to taste each of the three different foods per category, one at a time, taking note of the different tastes, feels, and colors. If possible, guide them through an orderly tasting session: *"Now let's all taste the plain cracker. . . whole wheat cracker . . . pumpernickel cracker. Now let's all take a sip of apple juice . . . cranberry juice . . . grape juice . . ."*

- Have children **DESCRIBE** what they are tasting based on:

    - salty, sweet, tart
    - dry, juicy
    - crunchy, soft

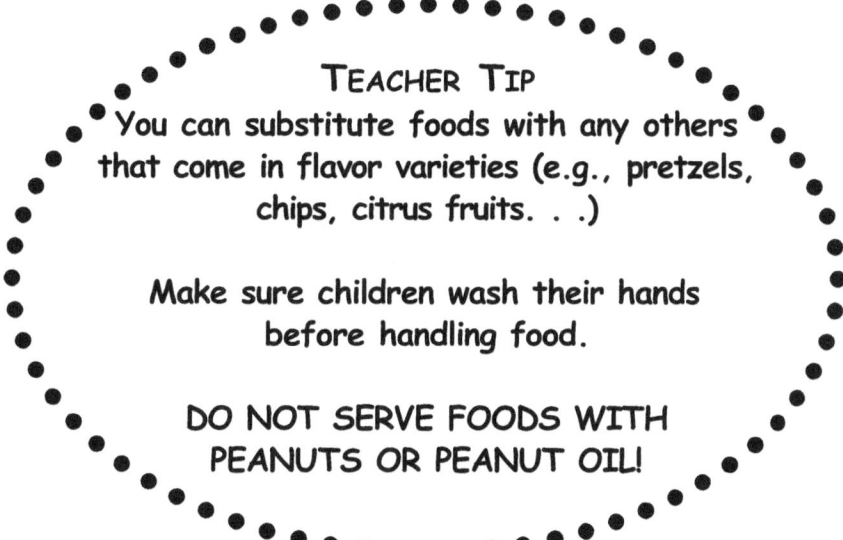

TEACHER TIP
You can substitute foods with any others that come in flavor varieties (e.g., pretzels, chips, citrus fruits. . .)

Make sure children wash their hands before handling food.

DO NOT SERVE FOODS WITH PEANUTS OR PEANUT OIL!

Hygiene/Self-Help

TAKE A TASTE
Tries New Food

MIND STRETCHERS

Budding Learners:
Describe foods during tasting to help budding learners identify them correctly: "The wheat cereal is light brown...the cranberry juice is red..."

Blossoming Learners:
Encourage blossoming learners to name other foods they know that taste similar to the buffet foods and juices.

Hygiene/Self-Help

TAKE A TASTE
Tries New Food

Activity 3
Flavor Favorites

Goal
Discover favorite foods

- **PREPARE** four poster boards, each with its own heading:

| Cereal | Crackers | Fruit | Juice |

- **COPY** templates on the following page and give to children along with scissors and colored markers.

- Children will color each of the foods with corresponding colors (e.g., white for rice cereal, yellow for corn cereal, brown for wheat cereal, etc.).

- One category at a time, children will indicate which was their favorite flavor in each. Have them hand you the food cut-out that represents their favorite in each category (rice, or corn, or wheat, for example).

- **CREATE** a picture bar graph of the children's favorite flavors. Now they can plainly see the classroom **FLAVOR FAVORITES** from the **FLAVOR BUFFET**. Display the boards where all can see!

CEREAL

Rice   Corn   Wheat

169

Hygiene/Self-Help

TAKE A TASTE
Tries New Food

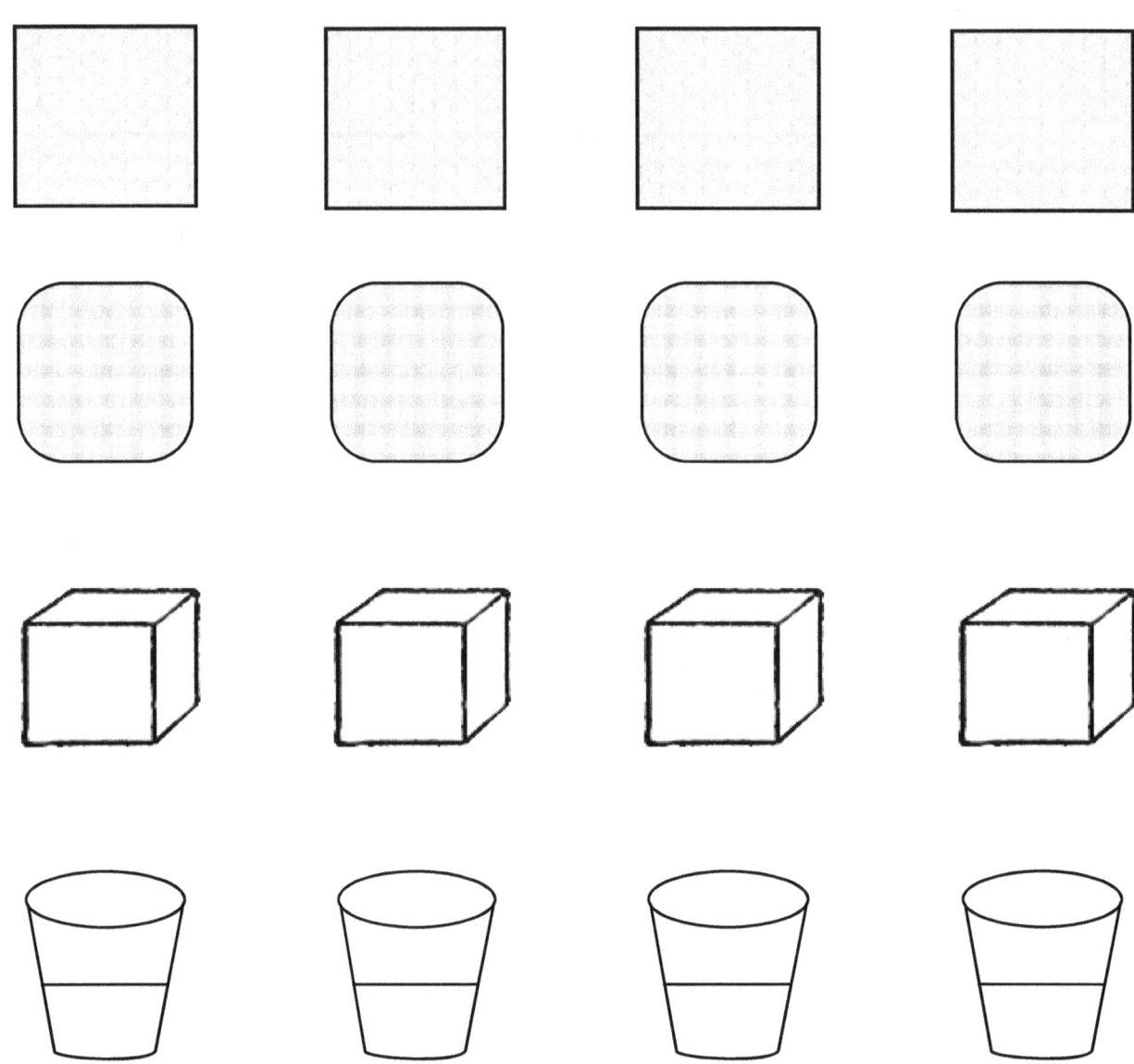

Hygiene/Self-Help

What's To Eat?

Identifies Food

Activity 1
Read *HOW ARE YOU PEELING?*
by Saxton Freyman and Joost Elffers

Goal
Identify foods by sight

Let's Read!

HOW ARE YOU PEELING? by Saxton Freyman and Joost Elffers is packed with photos of "Foods With Moods." Peeled, posed and looking quite alive, these fruit and veggie characters are more expressive then you'd think produce could be!

Other "Foods With Moods" books by Saxton Freyman and Joost Elffers include *PLAY WITH YOUR FOOD, PLAY WITH YOUR PUMPKINS, FAST FOOD, FOOD FOR THOUGHT*, and *DOG FOOD*. All are great choices for this activity.

Let's Talk!

- **READ** the book once through for the story and to let the art make a first impression.

- Page through the book again, this time **ASKING** children to identify the different foods used to create the characters.

- How many of these foods are familiar? How many are new? Allow children to share their experiences with favorite and not-so-favorite foods.

Teacher Tip
Bring in sliced veggies and fruits for children to sample as they talk about favorites, and new and different foods.
Be mindful of possible food allergies

Hygiene/Self-Help

What's To Eat?
Identifies Food

A Little Or A Lot

If it comes from Mother Nature
Like tomatoes, plums, or peas,
Yellow corn or sweet bananas,
You should EAT A LOT OF THESE.
Crispy lettuce, crunch carrots . . .
Go ahead and fill your dish.
These are foods that make you healthy.
Have as many as you wish!

If it doesn't grow in nature,
If it's filled with fat and oil,
If it's topped with sugar,
Then it's wrapped in plastic or in foil,
Like a donut or a cookie,
Or like candies, cakes or pies . . .
You should ONLY EAT A LITTLE BIT
Of these if you are wise.

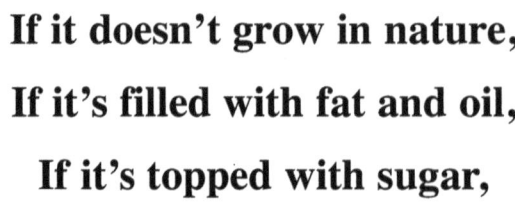

Hygiene/Self-Help

> ## WHAT'S TO EAT?
> **Identifies Food**
>
> **Activity 2**
> **Good-For-You Foods**
>
> **Goal**
> Differentiate between nutritious and non-nutritious foods

- **READ** the poem *A LITTLE OR A LOT* aloud two times.

- Ask children to recall the foods mentioned in the poem that are nutritious and will make them healthy.

- Next ask them to name the foods that are not so nutritious.

- Talk about what makes foods good for you or not-so-good for you.

    - Are foods that taste good always good for you?

    - Can some foods taste good but make you feel bad?

    - Why should you eat more foods that are good for you?

173

Hygiene/Self-Help

WHAT'S TO EAT?
Identifies Food

Activity 3
Play WHAT'S THE DISH?

Goal
Understand that certain foods should be eaten in moderation

- **USE** the reproducible on the following page to create sturdy display dishes. (It's best to laminate or reinforce with poster board.)

- **EXPLAIN** that nutritious foods can be eaten almost any time and in any amount (**HAVE AS MUCH AS YOU WISH!**) while non-nutritious foods should be eaten only once in a while and in much smaller portions (**USE A SMALL DISH!**)

- **HOLD** one plate in each hand and **INVITE** children to give examples of foods they like to eat. As each example is called out, **ASK** whether it's a food that should be eaten as much as you wish or if it's better to use a small dish. Hold up the corresponding dish as each correct answer is given.

- Next, have children **FILL** their own dishes. **USE** reproducibles to make individual copies for children to color with crayons or markers, then cut out with scissors.

- Children should **FILL** large dishes with pictures of nutritious as-much-as-you-wish foods. But only two or fewer non-nutritious items go on the small dish to show that we shouldn't eat as many of these.

MIND STRETCHERS

Budding Learners:
Budding learners may fill their big dish with a large amount of only one or two types of food that they know are nutritious.

Blossoming Learners:
Blossoming learners should be able to fill their big dish with a wider variety of nutritious foods.

Hygiene/Self-Help

What's To Eat?
Identifies Food

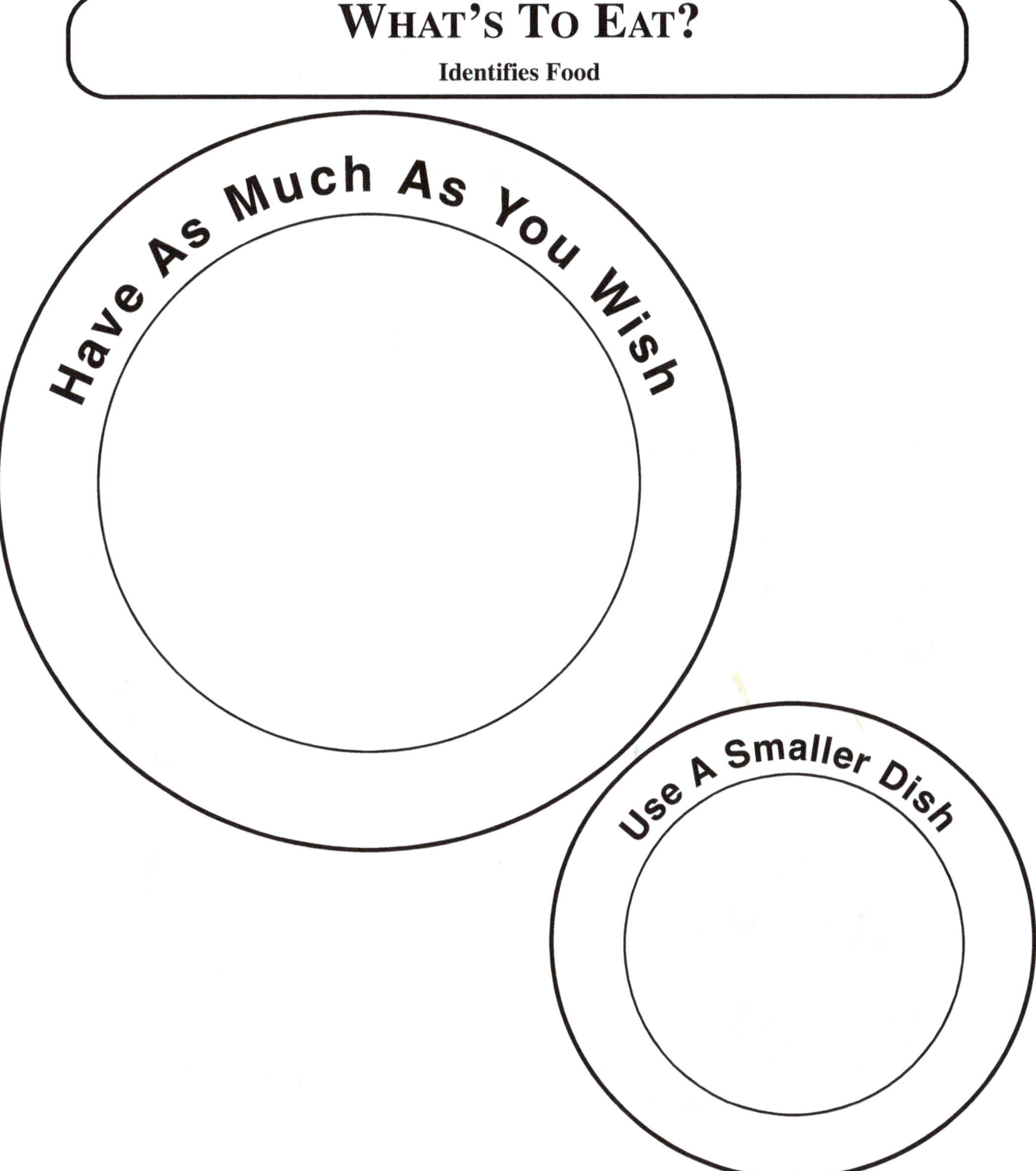

Have As Much As You Wish

Use A Smaller Dish

Hygiene/Self-Help

PLAY IT SAFE
Shows Safety Judgment

Activity 1
Make a Stop Sign

Goal
Understand how stop signs, and other safety signs, help us make smart safety choices

- **USE** Stop Sign reproducible on the next page to help children create their own safety patrol stop signs.

- **HAVE** children color and cut out stop sign faces and paste them onto Popsicle-stick handles.

- **TALK** about how stop signs help keep people safe on the roads.

- What other signs help us make smart safety choices?

Hygiene/Self-Help

PLAY IT SAFE
Shows Safety Judgment

Hygiene/Self-Help

> **PLAY IT SAFE**
>
> **Shows Safety Judgment**
>
> **Activity 1**
> **Safety Patrol**
>
> **Goal**
> Recognize situations that require extra attention to safety;
> know how to make smart safety choices

- In this activity, children will **HAVE FUN ACTING AS SAFETY PATROLS** as you read through the story of *ALEX AND THE PAPER SAILBOAT*.

- **INSTRUCT** children to wave their stop signs high in the air and shout out **"STOP!"** whenever they hear something in the story that's not safe. Their job is to step in whenever Alex is about to do something that requires better safety judgment.

- When the safety patrols yell **"STOP!"**, the teacher immediately stops reading and asks

    - "What is Alex doing wrong?"

    - "What should he do instead if he wants to stay safe?"

- The text is marked with a **stop sign icon** to indicate when in the story you should expect your safety patrols to interrupt.

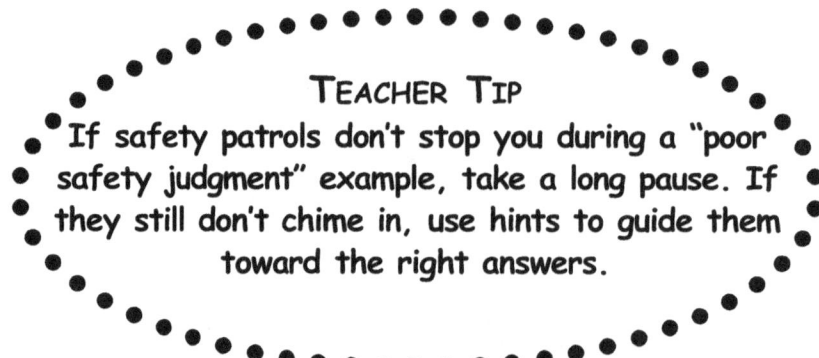

TEACHER TIP
If safety patrols don't stop you during a "poor safety judgment" example, take a long pause. If they still don't chime in, use hints to guide them toward the right answers.

Hygiene/Self-Help

Play It Safe
Shows Safety Judgment

Let's Read!

ALEX AND THE PAPER SAILBOAT

Alex was excited to make a paper sailboat. He found scissors in this arts-and-crafts box. He picked them up and ran downstairs to begin making his boat.

 **Alex should not run with scissors. He should hold them carefully, point facing down, and walk slowly while he's carrying them.**

Alex carefully cut the pieces of colored paper into the shape of a boat. Next he made a white sail. But as he was about to glue the sail into place, he noticed his glue bottle was empty.

"Where can I find more glue?" Alex wondered. He went to his father's workbench. There he found many bottles and cans of all different sizes. Alex wasn't sure what was inside them. He picked up a plastic bottle that looked like it might have glue inside. He began to open it.

 **Alex should not open bottles or cans if he doesn't know what's inside them. Some substances in the house, like cleaning fluids, can be dangerous! Alex should get help from a grown-up.**

Alex decided to ask his mother for some glue. He finished his paper sailboat. Then he waited for it to dry. Later, Alex took his sailboat outside to see if it would sail in the swimming pool in the back yard. Mom and Dad were busy gardening in the front yard.

179

Hygiene/Self-Help

Play It Safe
Shows Safety Judgment

Alex went out the back door and knelt down by the edge of the swimming pool. He reached over to set his boat in the water.

 **Alex should not play in or near a swimming pool by himself. Children should ONLY play by water if a grown-up is there to watch.**

Alex remembered Mom and Dad said *"never play by the swimming pool without a grown-up to watch you."* He decided to walk to the front yard to ask Mom and Dad to play with him.

On his way, Alex noticed a dog walking across his neighbor's lawn. The dog was not on a leash, and Alex had never seen him before. But the dog looked friendly. Alex thought about petting the dog on the head to find out if he was as soft as he looked.

 **Alex should never pet a dog he doesn't know. It may be a biting dog. Always ask a dog's owner before petting. Then carefully reach toward the dog with a closed hand (never open fingers) until you are sure it's a friendly dog.**

Just then, the dog's owner called the dog into the house. Alex said, "Oh well," and walked toward the front yard. He saw that his parents were across the street talking to the neighbors.

Alex could not wait to show his parents his new paper sailboat. He walked to the end of his driveway and began to walk into the street.

 **Alex should not cross the street before looking both ways to check for cars. Better yet, he should wait for his parents to help him across.**

Hygiene/Self-Help

PLAY IT SAFE
Shows Safety Judgment

"Stay there, Alex!" said Dad. "We're coming back across." And so Alex stayed on his side of the street.

Mom and Dad were very happy to see Alex's sailboat. "We love it!" said Dad.

"It's beautiful," said Mom. "Now let's all go to the pool together and see how it sails."

"What a great idea!" said Alex. And off they went to watch Alex's paper sailboat float across the water.

MIND STRETCHERS

Budding Learners:
Budding learners may know an action requires safety judgment, but may be slow to articulate safety rules. Give them plenty of time to explain.

Blossoming Learners:
Invite blossoming learners to give more examples of safety rules to be practiced at home or at school (e.g., Don't talk to strangers).

Hygiene/Self-Help

> ## How's The Weather?
> **Recognizes Weather**
>
> **Activity 1**
> **Seasonal Weather**
>
> **Goal**
> Know the weather for each season

Recite and Learn Seasons

- **READ** the verse below aloud two times before asking children to recite it with you.

- **CLAP** along with the beat to make the learning easier.

> # SEASONS
> Spring brings blossoms.
> Summer shines bright.
> Crispy Fall is colorful.
> Chilly Winter's white.

Talk about what the weather is like during each season:

- What kind of weather is needed to bring **BLOSSOMS**?

- What makes summer **BRIGHT**?

- What is **CRISPY** weather like?

- Why is fall **COLORFUL**?

- Why is winter **WHITE**?

182

Hygiene/Self-Help

How's The Weather?

Recognizes Weather

Activity 2
Birthday Seasons

Goal
Know what season birthday is in

Let's Draw!

- Children form groups based on their birthday seasons.

- Unroll 5-6 feet of mural paper and tape it horizontally along a wall.

- Give children crayons or colored markers and encourage each group to decorate their season with pictures of weather conditions, seasonal clothing, activities, holidays or symbols of the season.

Teacher Tip
To reinforce the concepts of weather and the seasons, review the "Tis The Season" section.

MIND STRETCHERS

Budding Learners:
Be sure to have a list of children's birthdays on hand. Budding learners may not know their birthday months or seasons.

Blossoming Learners:
Blossoming learners are likely to know the month and season of their birthday. Can they name the date and year they were born?

Hygiene/Self-Help

How's The Weather?

Recognizes Weather

Activity 3
Weather Match-Up Activity Sheet

Goal
Know which clothing and activities
are appropriate for each weather condition

Weather Match-Up

Which one doesn't belong?

Hygiene/Self-Help

COMING AND GOING

Understands Travel

Activity 1
How did I Get Here?

Goal
Understand that different people use different modes
of transportation at different times

LET'S SHARE!

- What are the different ways we get to and from school? (Examples: car, train, bus, bike, walking)

- What other kinds of transportation do people use? (Examples: planes, boats, motorcycles)

- Using the transportation reproducible on the next page, have kids color and cut out the picture that shows how they get to and from school.

- Create a new picture bar graph (like the one in the "Take a Taste" section) but this time showing different ways classmates travel to school.

- Discuss which modes of transportation are most used by the class. Which are the least used?

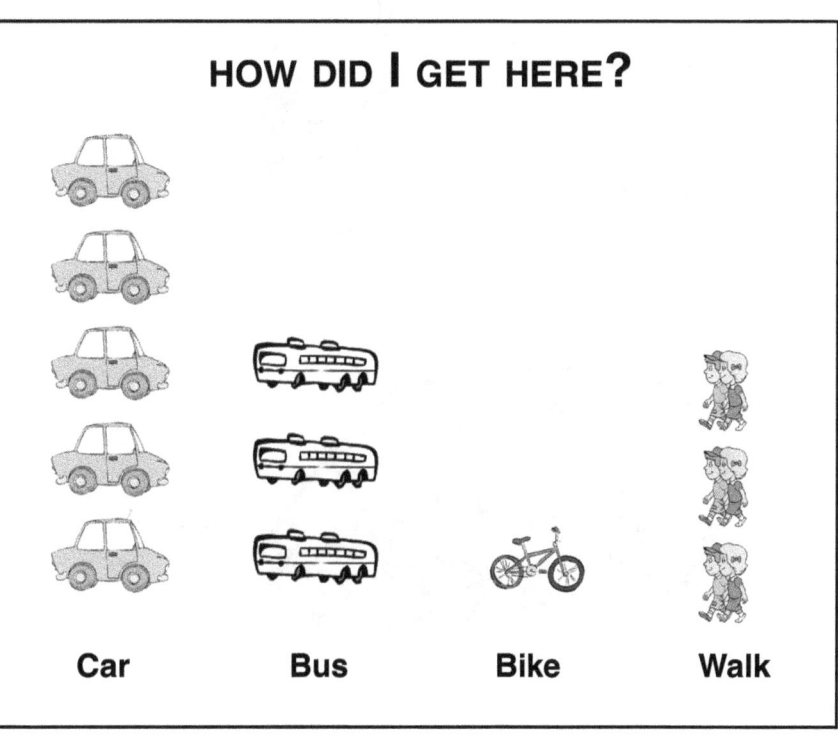

185

Hygiene/Self-Help

Coming And Going
Understands Travel

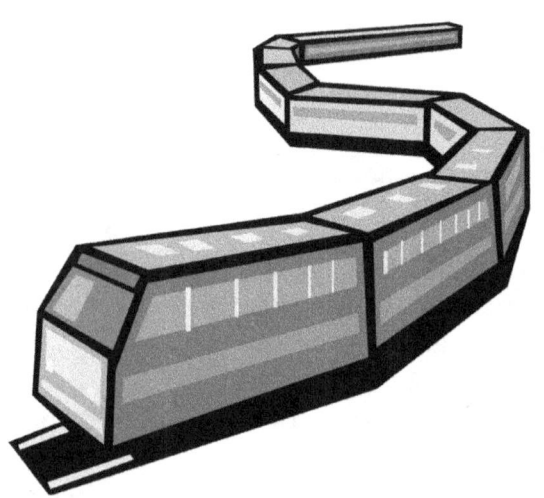

Hygiene/Self-Help

COMING AND GOING

Understands Travel

Activity 2
Travel Tips

Goal
Identify different modes of transportation by description

Read the verses aloud. Ask children to listen for travel tips in the verse. Then fill in the blank (by calling out answers) with the right form of transportation. For extra fun, make flash cards with pictures of the answers. Hold them up when the children guess correctly.

I have four tires under me.
I travel places near and far.
You guide me with a steering wheel.
You ride inside me. I'm a _____.

(Answer: car)

I'm tucked inside your walking shoes.
I take you up and down the street.
I'm at the bottom of your legs.
That's right! You guessed it -- I'm your _____.

(Answer: Feet)

I may be very, very big
And yet on water I can float.
I sail on rivers, lakes or seas.
Ahoy there, mates! I'm a _____.

(Answer: boat)

Sometimes I travel underground.
Sometimes outside in sun or rain.
I ride along the railroad tracks
For miles and miles. I'm a _____.

(Answer: train)

Hold tightly to my handlebars.
I'll take you anywhere you like.
Be sure to strap your helmet on
Each time your ride me. I'm your _____.

(Answer: bike)

I soar up high into the sky.
I travel faster than a train.
I have two wings and one long tail.
A pilot flies me. I'm a _____.

(Answer: plane)

Hygiene/Self-Help

COMING AND GOING
Understands Travel

MIND STRETCHERS

Budding Learners & Blossoming Learners

 All students should know the afternoon pick-up routine. Remind them to never leave the classroom until a parent (or other pick-up person) tells the teacher. Have blossoming learners take turns telling the pick-up rules. Do this at times other than pick-up time when there is a full class focus.

Hygiene/Self-Help

No Place Like Home
Knows Address And Phone Number

Mr. McPheet
Of Sycamore Street

Mr. McPheet lived on <u>Sycamore Street</u>
Half a block beyond <u>Appleton Way</u>.
On the days when it snowed
He would slide down the road
In his gleaming electric red sleigh.

He would slide right on through
to <u>Kazoo Avenue</u>
Past the park at the corner of <u>Main</u>.
Then he'd stop for some tea,
And a muffin or three,
On the south side of <u>Cherry Tree Lane</u>.

Hygiene/Self-Help

NO PLACE LIKE HOME
Knows Address And Phone Number

Activity 1
Street Smarts

Goal
Identify different ways to say street;
know name of street where home is located

● Read the Mr. McPheet poem two times aloud. Ask children to name all the different words for street that they hear. Read poem as many times as necessary for children to identify all street references.

- Street
- Way
- Road
- Avenue
- Lane

● Can you think of other words that mean street?

- Drive
- Boulevard
- Circle
- Court

● Ask each child in turn to name what street he or she lives on. Do you also know your street number?

Hygiene/Self-Help

No Place Like Home
Knows Address And Phone Number

Teacher Tip

Repeatedly reciting an address in a rhyming or sing-songy fashion will help a child memorize it more easily.

If a child's street name involves a visual image, help them draw a picture to represent their street name and include the house number.

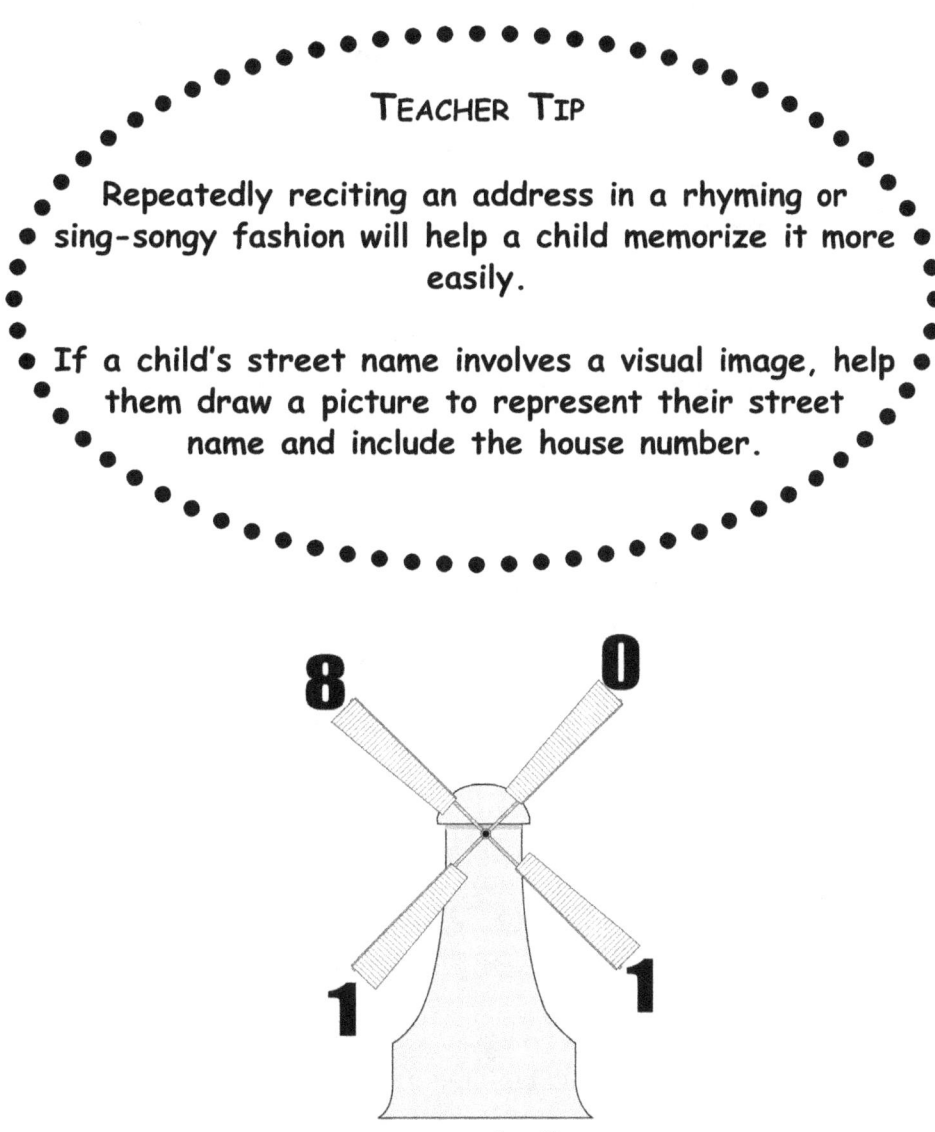

1801 Windmill Lane

A fun picture can help visual learners remember an address

Hygiene/Self-Help

> ## NO PLACE LIKE HOME
> **Knows Address And Phone Number**
>
> **Activity 2**
> **Where In The World**
>
> **Goal**
> Know city and state where home is located

LET'S LOCATE!

- **SHOW** children a picture (or mobile display) of our **SOLAR SYSTEM**. **ASK** "Where in the world do we live?"

- Help narrow down their choices by asking:

    - If we're on planet Mercury, are we home?
    - If we're on Mars, are we home?
    - If we're on planet earth, are we home?

- **REPEAT** the exercise using a globe and asking which **COUNTRY** we live in.

- Next, **SHOW** a US map. Help children locate their **STATE** on the map. You may need to include more than one state if you're located in a two- or tri-state area.

- **REPEAT** the exercise with **CITY** or **TOWN**, keeping in mind several may be represented. Some children may not know this answer. Keep a class address list on hand for this exercise.

- Use the reproducible on the next page so children can color in their home state on the USA map.

Hygiene/Self-Help

NO PLACE LIKE HOME
Knows Address And Phone Number

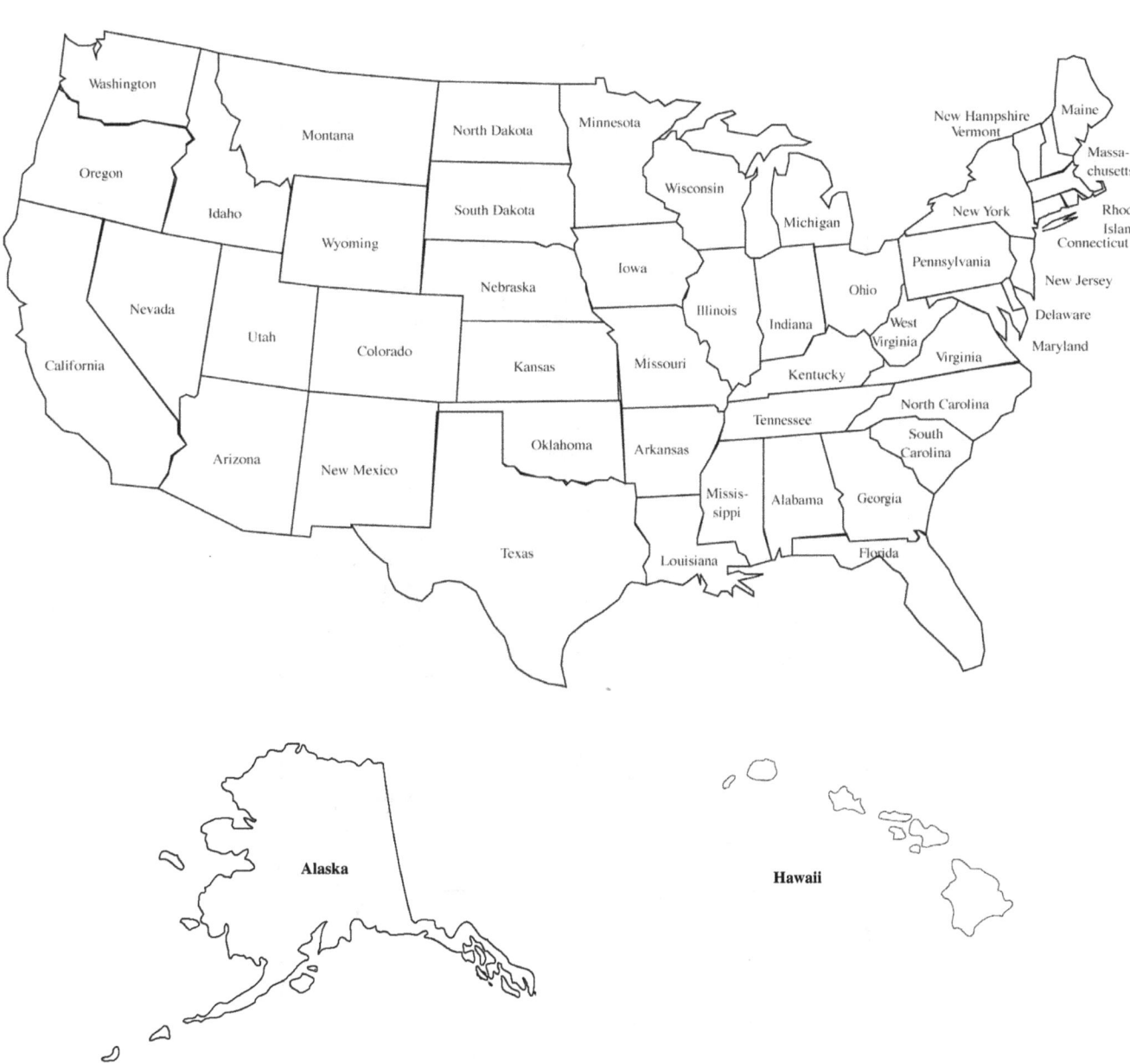

193

Hygiene/Self-Help

NO PLACE LIKE HOME
Knows Address And Phone Number

Hygiene/Self-Help

No Place Like Home

Knows Address And Phone Number

Activity 3
Phone Home

Goal
Memorize home phone number

- **USE** the reproducible on the preceding page to help children become familiar with the phone.

- Help them color in the numbers on the keypad that are in their home phone number, or the number of a responsible adult.

- **REPEAT** the exercise using a globe and asking which **COUNTRY** we live in.

- Next, they can write out the seven-digit phone number on the display screen. Many may need help with this.

Teacher Tip
Address/Phone Safety

Remind children not to give out address or phone information without their Mom or Dad's okay.

EXCEPTION: It's okay to give your phone number to a police officer who can help you call home if you ever get lost.

NEVER give the information to strangers.

Hygiene/Self-Help

No Place Like Home
Knows Address And Phone Number

MIND STRETCHERS

Budding Learners:
Use a class contact list. Budding learners are not likely to know their street or phone numbers. Use a simple tune to help them learn the numbers.

Blossoming Learners:
Blossoming learners who already know their seven-digit phone numbers may be ready to learn their three-digit area codes too.

Hygiene/Self-Help

> ## READY TO WEAR
> **Dresses Self**
>
> **Activity 1**
> **Read and Discuss *STOP THOSE PANTS!* by Mordicai Gerstein**
>
> **Goal**
> Know which articles of clothing make a complete outfit;
> talk about morning dressing routine

LET'S READ!

In *STOP THOSE PANTS!* by Mordicai Gerstein, a mischievous pair of pants brings laughs and mayhem to a little boy's morning dressing routine.

This story gets young children talking about the challenges of finding all the right pieces of an outfit -- from underwear, shirt and pants to socks and shoes -- and getting everything on just right!

LET'S TALK!

- How many pieces of clothing did Murray put on? Count aloud as you name each piece: 1 pair of underwear, 1 shirt, 1 pair of jeans, 2 socks, 2 shoes

- Why didn't the pants want Murray to wear them?

- How did Murray get his pants to cooperate?

- Where was Murray's left shoe? Do you ever misplace a shoe? Can you tie your shoes by yourself?

- What's the trickiest part about getting dressed by yourself?

- What's the best part about getting dressed by yourself?

Hygiene/Self-Help

Ready To Wear
Dresses Self

Activity 2
Play Dress-Up Time

Goal
Practice working with buttons, zippers and ties

- Provide a selection of costumes and clothes (adult- and kid-size)

- Children can choose a person they want to dress like (mom, dad, teacher, big brother/sister, doctor, fire fighter . . . even Murray!)

- Help with tricky fasteners, such as buttons, zippers and snaps. Be sure to guide them through the process rather than doing it for them.

- When all children are dressed, have them walk around the classroom in a dress-up costume parade.

- For extra fun, use an instant camera and snap pictures to send home.

Teacher Tip

Before starting, remind children to put costume pieces on over their own clothing.

Be sure to include several clothing pieces that have buttons, zippers, snaps, hook, and ties.

Hygiene/Self-Help

READY TO WEAR
Dresses Self

Activity 3
SHOE-PER STAR!

Goal
Ties own shoes

- Practice shoe tying with children until they're able to tie their laces by themselves.

- Create a SHOE-PER STAR display by cutting out a large piece of sturdy poster board into the shape of a star.

- Display the star in a special place in the classroom.

- As children become able to tie their own shoes unassisted, write their name on a shoe, using the reproducible on the next page.

- Have the new SHOE-PER STAR color their shoe with crayons or markers.

- Then add it to the I'm a SHOE-PER STAR display!

MIND STRETCHERS

Budding Learners:
Try "bunny ears" shoe tying with budding learners. Make two loops, cross one over the other, wrap it around and under, and pull both tight.

Blossoming Learners:
Blossoming learners can try the one-loop wrap, making sure to use their dominant hand to put the one lace under and tie a half-knot.

Hygiene/Self-Help

Ready To Wear
Dresses Self

Hygiene/Self-Help

> ## TABLE TOOLS
> **Uses Spoon And Fork**
>
> **Activity 1**
> **Self-Serve Snack Bar**
>
> **Goal**
> Know how to successfully manipulate spoon and form

LET'S EAT!

Have a special snack-time **SELF-SERVE SNACK BAR!**

- **FILL** a bowl with pre-sliced bananas (1 large banana per 2-3 students) and a large serving spoon.

- **SET** a table with plastic spoons, plastic forks, small disposable bowls, small paper plates, and napkins.

- **PLACE** all food items on table, along with large serving spoons for each item.

    - serving bowl of banana slices
    - serving bowl of applesauce
    - container of non-dairy shipped topping

- **INVITE** children to serve themselves (using large spoons) at the snack bar. **OBSERVE** their skill at manipulating serving spoons. **RESIST** the temptation to serve for them, unless they clearly need help.

- As children eat, **REMIND** them to enjoy their food by using forks for banana slices and spoons for applesauce . . . and, of course, napkins for small messes.

Hygiene/Self-Help

TABLE TOOLS

Uses Spoon And Fork

Activity 1
Table Tool Art

Goal
Know which utensils to use for which foods

LET'S EAT!

- **USE** the reproducible on the next page to make Table Tool Art. Give children crayons or markers to draw right on the plate and inside the bowl.

- **FILL** the bowl with food(s) that you use a spoon to eat (soup, cereal, ice cream, pudding).

- **FILL** the plate with foods that require a fork.

- **DISPLAY** the finished pictures and talk as a group about different foods we know that require forks or spoons.

MIND STRETCHERS

Budding Learners:
Don't allow budding learners to struggle or become frustrated with serving spoons. Help if necessary, and make light of minor spills or messes.

Blossoming Learners:
Blossoming learners can get more practice by serving budding learners who have difficulty manipulating the larger utensils.

Hygiene/Self-Help

TABLE TOOLS
Uses Spoon And Fork

Common Core Standards Correlations

NATIONAL CHILD ASSESSMENT FORM
TEACHING TERRIFIC FIVES AND OTHER CHILDREN

This document is a correlation of the skills presented in the *Teaching Terrific Fives and Other Children* to the skills that are assessed on the National Child Assessment Form. This assessment form is used to determine whether students are ready both developmentally and intellectually to move into kindergarten. This correlation indicates where the skills that will be assessed are presented in this book.

Social Economic Development

1. Identifies body parts
2. Shows feeling 44-51
3. Separates from parents
4. Relates to adults
5. Interacts with children 40-43
6. Seeks new experiences
7. Maintains interest
8. Plays cooperatively
9. Modulates voice
10. Persists in task
11. Shows pride
12. Shows social awareness
13. Protects self 10-15
14. Concerned about fairness 16-20
15. Demonstrates responsibility 21-24
16. Aware of consequences 25-30
17. Shows creativity 31-35
18. Exhibits appropriate values 36-39

Language Development

19. Follows directions
20. Extended listening 24
21. Follows directions
22. Discriminates between words
23. Labels objects
24. Speaks informally 100-105
25. Initiates conversation
26. Speaks more extensively
27. Asks questions
28. Uses prepositions

29. Uses adjectives ....
30. Exhibits auditory memory ....
31. Sequencing and retelling 54-58
32. Exhibits reading interest 59-62
33. Knows reading progression 63-66
34. Knows alphabet 67-79
35. Uses imagination 81-84
36. Plays roles 85-91

Cognitive Development

37. Visual discrimination with colors ....
38. Identifies shapes 136-139
39. Classifies objects 114
40. Understands number concepts ....
41. Knows the five senses ....
42. Draws a person (outline) 112
43. Compares length ....
44. Compares size ....
45. Understands numbers ....
46. Detects a pattern ....
47. Understands relative qualities ....
48. Understands numbers ....
49. Knows seasons 108-111
50. Draws a person (details) 113, 160-163
51. Classifies objects (matching set to use) 115
52. Recognizes fantasy 116-117
53. Recognizes cause and effect 120-121
54. Predicts outcomes 122-126

Motor Skills Development

55. Walks on tiptoes ....
56. Walks balance board ....
57. Jumps from stool ....
58. Hops on one foot ....
59. Catches ball (12" diameter) 152-153
60. Throws ball 152-153
61. Balances on one foot ....
62. Works puzzle (3 pieces) 134-135
63. Copies a circle and a cross ....
64. Gallops 151
65. Dances ....
66. Explores space ....
67. Works puzzle (5 pieces) 136-139
68. Uses scissors 100-105, 136-139
69. Copies letters 140-148, 156-159
70. Skips 149-150

71. Catches ball (3-4" diameter) 152-153
72. Walks backward 154-155

Hygiene and Self-Development

73. Allows sufficient time for toilet needs ....
74. Dresses self (basic) 197
75. Knows identifying information ....
76. Uses spoon and fork 201-203
77. Puts things away ....
78. Cleans spills ....
79. Plays actively ....
80. Manages bathroom facilities ....
81. Dresses self (buttons and zippers) 198-200
82. Helps prepare for activity ....
83. Cares for toys ....
84. Cares for possessions ....
85. Tries new food 166-179
86. Identifies food 171-175
87. Demonstrates judgment 176-181
88. Recognizes weather 182-184
89. Understands travel 185-188
90. Knows address and telephone number 189-196

HEAD START KINDERGARTEN READINESS ASSESSMENT
TEACHING TERRIFIC FIVES AND OTHER CHILDREN

A. Academics

1. Recognizes letters 140-148, 156-159
2. Recognizes shapes 134-136
3. Recognizes colors ....
4. Counts 10 objects ....
5. Writes own first name ....
6. Can recognize rhyming words ....

B. Self-Regulation

1. Comforts self 10-15
2. Pays attention ....
3. Controls impulses ....
4. Follow directions ....
5. Negotiates solutions ....
6. Plays cooperatively ....
7. Plays cooperatively ....
8. Plays cooperatively ....

C. Social Expression

1. Expresses empathy ....
2. Relates well to adults ....
3. Has expressive abilities ....
4. Is curious and eager to learn ....
5. Expresses needs and wants ....
6. Engages in symbolic play 85-91

D. Self-Care and Motor Skills

1. Use of small manipulatives ....
2. Has general coordination 24, 149-155
3. Performs basic self-help/self-care tasks 197-200

Humanics National Child Assessment Form

Humanics National Child Assessment Form

Three to Six

Marsha Kaufman, Ph.D., and T. Thomas McMurrain, Ph.D.

ABOUT THE FORM
The Humanics National Child Assessment Form is a checklist of skills and behaviors a child is likely to develop from three to six years of age. Each item in the checklist is a sample of many related skills and behaviors and in that sense serves as an index of more general characteristics of development. Items in the Assessment From are grouped into five scales that represent areas of child development: **Social-Emotional, Motor Skills, Language, Cognitive,** and **Hygiene/Self-Help**.

Within each scale, the items are arranged in a developmental sequence, and space is provided for assessing the child four different times during the year. The Child Development Profile allows a visual representation of the child's ratings on each scale at the time of each assessment.

A NOTE TO THE PARENT
No one knows more about the development of your child than you do. This checklist is to structure some topics you and the teacher will discuss about your child. You may often want to add your own opinions and observations about your child's development. The information you and the teacher share is very important in designing an educational experience which will respond to and stimulate the individual nature and personality of your child.

DIRECTIONS
Complete all the items in the Assessment Form by observing the child in everyday play activities, or, if necessary, structuring special "testing" situations to let you observe the described behavior.

Score each item as follows:

Make No Check Mark—	If the characteristic is not present or the behavior does not occur.
Check in the "Occurs Occasionally" Column—	If the characteristic or behavior is sometimes present, but it is not a consistent part of the behavior. The behavior has occurred occasionally but is not firmly mastered or developed.
Check in the "Occurs Consistently" Column—	If the characteristic or behavior has been mastered and occurs consistently as a part of the child's behavior.

The Humanics National Child Assessment Form is designed to help the teacher observe the child in different areas of development and to follow changes over the years. It is to be used as a tool in planning educational and developmental experiences for the child. The form is intended to be used by teachers and parents to better understand and relate to the individual needs of the child.

© 1982 by Humanics, Ltd.
Revised 2000
Copyright © 2000 by Brumby Holdings, Inc.

All rights reserved. No part of this book may be reproduced or used in any form or by any means-graphic, electronic, or mechanical—including photocopying, recording, taping, or information storage and retrieval systems—without permission from the publisher.

800-874-8844   In State 404-874-1930   Fax 404-874-1976   www.humanicslearning.com

Humanics National Child Assessment Form

SOCIAL EMOTIONAL

Social-Emotional	Expressing feelings and interacting with others. This includes, among other characteristics, expressing and controlling feelings, cooperating with others, showing social awareness, self-concept development, relationship to parents and relationship to adults in general.	Date____ Occurs Occasionally	Occurs Consistently	Date____ Occurs Occasionally	Occurs Consistently	Date____ Occurs Occasionally	Occurs Consistently	Date____ Occurs Occasionally	Occurs Consistently
1. Identifies Body Parts	Points on request to face, arm leg or foot								
2. Shows Feelings	Smiles and shows other appropriate emotional responses								
3. Separates from Parents	Separates from parent without reluctance								
4. Relates to Adults	Calls by name two adults on staff; relates positively to adults but is not overly dependent								
5. Interacts with Children	Talks comfortably with other children								
6. Seeks New Experiences	Eager for and seeks out new activities and experiences; exhibits curiosity								
7. Maintains Interest	Maintains interest in play activity without encouragement from an adult								
8. Plays Cooperatively	Plays cooperatively in groups of three or four children								
9. Modulates Voice	Controls volume of speech when directed and when participating in singing and language games								
10. Persists in Task	Stays actively involved in a chosen task until completed or for at least fifteen minutes								

Humanics National Child Assessment Form

11.	Shows Pride	Shows pride in accomplishments or products created; exhibits confidence in own ability to accomplish simple tasks
12.	Shows Social Awareness	Shows awareness and respect for desires of other children
13.	Protects Self	Stands up for own rights and does not permit other children to constantly take unfair advantage
14.	Concerned About Fairness	Has a concern for fairness in what happens to other children
15.	Demonstrates Responsibility	Takes responsibility for own behavior in staying within the rules of games and activities
16.	Aware of Consequences	Behaves with an awareness of likely consequences of the behavior
17.	Shows Creativity	Contributes original ideas and exhibits flexibility in play and creation of products
18.	Exhibits Appropriate Values	Exhibits consideration for others, a sense of humor and self-discipline

COMMENTS AND NOTES:

Humanics National Child Assessment Form

LANGUAGE

Language	Developing communication skills. This includes such skills as listening, following directions, memory, self-expression, and reading interest	Date:___ Occurs Occasionally	Occurs Consistently	Date:___ Occurs Occasionally	Occurs Consistently	Date:___ Occurs Occasionally	Occurs Consistently	Date:___ Occurs Occasionally	Occurs Consistently
19. Follows Directions (I)	Follows a simple direction ("Sit down," "Jump," "Clap Hands," etc.)								
20. Extended Listening	Attends to a short story which is read directly, or played on tape or record								
21. Follows Directions (II)	Follows three or more successive directions in order								
22. Discriminates Between Words	Identifies similarity or difference between five pairs of words presented orally								
23. Labels Objects	Names objects in the environment								
24. Speaks Informally	Speaks effectively in short conversations and in response to questions								
25. Initiates Conversations	Takes leadership role in beginning a conversation								
26. Speaks More Extensively	Holds a conversations, or shares a report, which lasts for one or two minutes								
27. Asks Questions	Asks questions appropriate to the situation								
28. Uses Prepositions	Uses prepositions in describing relationships of one object to another								

Humanics National Child Assessment Form

29.	Uses Adjectives	Understands and uses adjectives and contrast words (opposites) correctly						
30.	Exhibits Auditory Memory	Repeats song or finger play from memory						
31.	Sequencing and Retelling	Retells a simple story in sequence						
32.	Exhibits Reading Interest	"Reads" a picture story book						
33.	Knows Reading Progression	Knows and exhibits appropriate reading progressions from left to right and top to bottom						
34.	Knows Alphabet	Recognizes and names the letters of the alphabet on sight						
35.	Uses Imagination	Can use imagination to create a simple story with some logical sequence						
36.	Plays Roles	Play activity involves pretending to be another recognizable person (e.g., I am a fireman, nurse, etc.)						

COMMENTS AND NOTES:

Humanics National Child Assessment Form

COGNITIVE

Cognitive	Acquiring and using information. This involves processes such as thinking, learning information, memory, imagination, problem solving and understanding.	Date_____ Occurs Occasionally	Occurs Consistently	Date_____ Occurs Occasionally	Occurs Consistently	Date_____ Occurs Occasionally	Occurs Consistently	Date_____ Occurs Occasionally	Occurs Consistently
37. Visual Discrimination with Colors	Differentiates between four similarly shaped objects by noting their differences in color								
38. Identifies Shapes	Identifies the following shapes: circles, square rectangle, and triangle								
39. Classifies Shapes (I)	Sorts objects into sets, matching objects according to color, shape, or size								
40. Understands Number Concepts (I)	Understands the number concept "one;" recognizes and names the numeral "1" on sight								
41. Knows the Five Senses	Can name the body part(s) associated with the five sense: eg., "We see with our eyes."								
42. Draws a Person (I)	Draws a human figure with head, body arms, and legs								
43. Compares Length	Selects longer of two sticks								
44. Compares Size	Selects biggest and smallest from four sizes of balls								
45. Understands Number Concepts (II)	Understand number concepts to five								
46. Detects a Pattern	Copies a pattern based on color, size or shape in stringing beads or stacking blocks								

214

Humanics National Child Assessment Form

47.	Understands Relative Qualities	Demonstrates understanding of relative qualities in such pairs of words as heavy and light, hot and cold, and fast and slow						
48.	Understands Number Concepts (III)	Understands number concepts to ten						
49.	Knows Seasons	Knows season of the year and how they relate to events and holidays (e.g., "School is out for most of the summer.")						
50.	Draws Person (I)	Draws human figure with details (fingers, toes, hands, ears, etc.)						
51.	Classifies Objects (II)	Sorts objects into sets, matching them according to use						
52.	Recognizes Fantasy	Can distinguish between fantasy and reality						
53.	Recognizes Cause and Effect	Shows awareness of the relationship between an action and its cause						
54.	Predicts Outcomes	Anticipates the consequences of simples actions						

COMMENTS AND NOTES:

Humanics National Child Assessment Form

MOTOR SKILLS

Motor Skills	Using the body with control and efficiency. This consists of fine motor skills such as cutting with scissors or copying with a pen, and gross motor skills such as walking, balancing, and jumping.	Date_____ Occurs Occasionally	Occurs Consistently	Date_____ Occurs Occasionally	Occurs Consistently	Date_____ Occurs Occasionally	Occurs Consistently	Date_____ Occurs Occasionally	Occurs Consistently
55. Walks on Tip Toes	Can walk on tip toes for four to five steps								
56. Walks Balance Board	Walks a balance board 6" wide, 3" off the ground								
57. Jumps from Stool	Jumps from 12" high object without falling								
58. Hops on One Foot	Hops on one foot at least three times in succession (3 years)								
59. Catches Ball (I)	Catches bounced ball (12" diameter) in arms								
60. Throw Ball	Throw three inch ball in generally intended direction								
61. Balances on One Foot	Balances on one foot for a slow count of three								
62. Works Puzzle (I)	Can put together a three-piece puzzle								
63. Copies a Circle and a Cross	Copies a circle drawing a single line and returning to general point of beginning; Copies a cross								
64. Gallops	Gallops continuously for a limited distance (4 years)								

Humanics National Child Assessment Form

65.	Dances	Dances with sense of rhythm
66.	Explores Space	Explores space by moving in several directions
67.	Works Puzzle (II)	Can successfully assemble a simple five-piece puzzle
68.	Uses Scissors	Uses scissors smoothly and with moderate control; cuts on a drawn line
69.	Copies Letters	Copies large capital letters
70.	Skips	Skips continuously for a defined distance (5 to 6 years)
71.	Catches Ball (II)	Catches 3" to 4" thrown ball just using hands
72.	Walks Backwards	Can walk backwards in a defined space without bumping others

COMMENTS AND NOTES:

Humanics National Child Assessment Form

HYGIENE/SELF-HELP

Hygiene and Self-Help	Caring for personal needs in healthy ways. This includes recognizing needs, accepting responsibility for satisfying needs and being able to take care of self in generally safe and accepted ways.	Date_____ Occurs Occasionally	Occurs Consistently	Date_____ Occurs Occasionally	Occurs Consistently	Date_____ Occurs Occasionally	Occurs Consistently	Date_____ Occurs Occasionally	Occurs Consistently
73. Allows Sufficient Time for Toilet Needs	Alerts teacher of needs. Controls need until toilet is used								
74. Dresses Self (I)	Puts on basic clothing such as shirts, pants, and socks without adult supervision								
75. Knows Identifying Information	Knows own first and last name, age and sex								
76. Uses Spoon and Fork	Eats with spoon or fork according to the type of food served								
77. Puts things Away	Follows directions in putting things away								
78. Cleans Spills	Cleans up spills with direction from teacher								
79. Plays Actively	Plays actively on the playground without the teacher's constant supervision								
80. Manages Bathroom Facilities	Manages bathroom facilities according to conventional routine								
81. Dresses Self (II)	Is able to manipulate buttons, zippers and other fasteners, and to tie shoes								
82. Helps Prepare for Activity	Helps set out project materials on table								

Humanics National Child Assessment Form

83.	Cares for Toys	Takes care of toys and materials					
84.	Cares for Possessions	Shows responsibility for personal possessions					
85.	Tries New Food	Samples a "taste test" of new food when it is served					
86.	Identifies Food	Classifies food belonging to the four basic food groups					
87.	Demonstrates Judgement	Exhibits proper judgement and understands safety principles					
88.	Recognizes Weather	Understands weather concepts; identifies play activities suitable for weather conditions, and dresses appropriately for the weather					
89.	Understands Travel	Locates classroom in the morning; knows afternoon pick-up procedure					
90.	Knows Address and Telephone Number	Knows home address or can tell where home is located; knows telephone number for home or responsible adult					

COMMENTS AND NOTES:

Humanics National Child Assessment Form

PLANNING: Use the information from individual items in the checklist and the Summary Profile Sheet to focus on the child's strength and readiness for new experiences. Items checked, "Occurs Occasionally" in the checklist are clues to readiness for experiences checked "Occurs Occasionally" in the checklist are clues to the readiness for experiences related to that item. Use the Planning Sheets to record specific areas of focus and activities for the child.

First Assessment _____

Strengths _____

Follow-up Activities Planned _____

Second Assessment _____

Areas of Demonstrated Improvement _____

Needs Support _____

Humanics National Child Assessment Form

Third Assessment _____

Areas of Demonstrated Improvement _____

Needs Support _____

Follow-up Activities Planned _____

Fourth Assessment _____

Areas of Demonstrated Improvement _____

Needs Support _____

Follow-up Activities Planned _____

Humanics National Child Assessment Form

CHILD DEVELOPMENT SUMMARY PROFILE

INSTRUCTIONS: Circle each item checked "Occurs Consistently" in each sub-scale (Social-Emotional, Language, Cognitive, Motor Skills, and Hygiene/Self-Help) using one color. Circle each item checked "Occurs Occasionally" in each sub-scale in another color on the chart below.

1st ASSESSMENT	Date _____ Teacher _____
SOCIAL-EMOTIONAL	1 2 3 4 5 6 7 8 9 10 11 12 13 14 15 16 17 18
LANGUAGE	19 20 21 22 23 24 25 26 27 28 29 30 31 32 33 34 35 36
COGNITIVE	37 38 39 40 41 42 43 44 45 46 47 48 49 50 51 52 53 54
GROSS MOTOR	55 56 57 58 59 60 61 62 63 64 65 66 67 68 69 70 71 72
FINE MOTOR	73 74 75 76 77 78 79 80 81 82 83 84 85 86 87 88 89 90

2nd ASSESSMENT	Date _____ Teacher _____
SOCIAL-EMOTIONAL	1 2 3 4 5 6 7 8 9 10 11 12 13 14 15 16 17 18
LANGUAGE	19 20 21 22 23 24 25 26 27 28 29 30 31 32 33 34 35 36
COGNITIVE	37 38 39 40 41 42 43 44 45 46 47 48 49 50 51 52 53 54
GROSS MOTOR	55 56 57 58 59 60 61 62 63 64 65 66 67 68 69 70 71 72
FINE MOTOR	73 74 75 76 77 78 79 80 81 82 83 84 85 86 87 88 89 90

3rd ASSESSMENT	Date _____ Teacher _____
SOCIAL-EMOTIONAL	1 2 3 4 5 6 7 8 9 10 11 12 13 14 15 16 17 18
LANGUAGE	19 20 21 22 23 24 25 26 27 28 29 30 31 32 33 34 35 36
COGNITIVE	37 38 39 40 41 42 43 44 45 46 47 48 49 50 51 52 53 54
GROSS MOTOR	55 56 57 58 59 60 61 62 63 64 65 66 67 68 69 70 71 72
FINE MOTOR	73 74 75 76 77 78 79 80 81 82 83 84 85 86 87 88 89 90

4th ASSESSMENT	Date _____ Teacher _____
SOCIAL-EMOTIONAL	1 2 3 4 5 6 7 8 9 10 11 12 13 14 15 16 17 18
LANGUAGE	19 20 21 22 23 24 25 26 27 28 29 30 31 32 33 34 35 36
COGNITIVE	37 38 39 40 41 42 43 44 45 46 47 48 49 50 51 52 53 54
GROSS MOTOR	55 56 57 58 59 60 61 62 63 64 65 66 67 68 69 70 71 72
FINE MOTOR	73 74 75 76 77 78 79 80 81 82 83 84 85 86 87 88 89 90

Humanics National Child Assessment Form

www.ingramcontent.com/pod-product-compliance
Lightning Source LLC
Chambersburg PA
CBHW080538170426
43195CB00016B/2601